Colorado's HISTORIC

Mountain PASSES

LARRY RYNEARSON • RICK JONES

*To, Vera + Kevin Larry Rynearson
Enjoy*

WESTERN REFLECTIONS PUBLISHING COMPANY®

Lake City, Colorado

© 2014 Larry Rynearson (text) and Rick Jones (photography)
All rights reserved. No part of this book may be reproduced in any form without permission in writing from the author.

ISBN 978-1-937851-19-4

Cover and book design: Laurie Goralka Design
Photography by Rick Jones unless otherwise noted.
Cover photograph: West side of Mosquito Pass

First Edition
Printed in Canada

Western Reflections Publishing Company®
P.O. Box 1149, 951 N. Highway 149
Lake City, CO 81235
(970) 944-0110
publisher@westernreflectionspublishing.com
www.westernreflectionspublishing.com

INTRODUCTION

and older boys went west after hearing about gold, silver, abundant wildlife, and free land. Soon prairie schooners filled with their women, children and possessions followed. Tent city mining camps sprung up overnight. Saloons, stores, boarding houses, and buildings for lawyers, doctors, and construction people turned camps into towns. Other settlers started farms and ranches to provide food for man and animals.

Put yourself in their place and ask if you could do what they did. They did not have modern conveniences and comforts. They did not have insulated and waterproof Sorel boots, vibram soled shoes, Gore-Tex clothing, polar fleece, and down jackets. Transportation in the high country was by foot and, if you were lucky, by mule or horse. Sleeping was in a canvas tent. A good day's travel might be ten miles, and all the while they were exposed to the elements.

High country road building started in the spring as soon as the snowmelt allowed access and continued through the summer until snow and cold weather made working impossible. In the winter, deep snow, frozen ground, high winds, and sub-zero temperatures made work impractical and unsafe. Spring and fall brought on the problem of rock slides. When daytime temperatures rise above freezing and night temperatures fall below freezing, a freeze/thaw cycle exists. During the day water seeps into cracks and weak areas in the rock. At night the water freezes and puts pressure in the cracks and expands them. As this cycle continues over time, the cracks get larger allowing more water to seep into the cracks. As this greater amount of water freezes, the ice expands putting greater pressure on the inside of the cracks. Eventually the rock is split off, often causing an unexpected and unpredictable rock slide.

The road builders did not have Caterpillar tractors and other powered equipment. They used handtools such as sledge hammers, picks, shovels, and dynamite. Trees for railroad ties, lumber, firewood, and mine timbers were cut by handsaws and axes and were moved by wagons and mules. Today these passes are used by U.S. and Colorado highways, country roads and forest roads throughout our state.

Chapter One will introduce you to the geography and geology of Colorado. In Chapter Two you will meet the state's earliest human residents. Chapters Three, Four, and Five are about people who worked to make settlement possible for others. The main reason for Colorado's rapid growth is the story of the "Mineral Belt" explained in Chapter Six. Chapter Seven is the story of our first railroads and how they made travel more comfortable and the movement of materials less expensive. Next we will cover the history of the individual passes.

The area of Colorado covered in the book is defined by the Wyoming state line on the north, Interstate Highway 25 on the east, the New Mexico state line on the south, and the Utah state line on the west.

The time frame of history in the book generally extends from the late 1850s to the beginning of World War I. Some information about events occurring after that war may be included if important to the history of a pass.

Introduction

Colorado is blessed with its history, culture, climate, and landscape. The wealth of its mineral deposits built and supported our mining industry. Skiing and tourism bring a large contribution to Colorado's economy. All of this is linked to the Rocky Mountains. The Rockies cross the middle of the state from the north to the south. They rise abruptly out of the eastern plains and subside in the plateaus of western Colorado.

The Colorado Rocky Mountains are one segment of the North American Rockies which start in Alaska and end in Mexico. Their origins are the result of long, slow collisions between two or more plates of the earth's crust. Some of these plates include the land masses we call continents. These rigid plates are in slow but constant motion propelled by the sea of molten rock below them. When this motion between plates results in a collision, pressures build to a point causing fractures of uplifts and folds to relieve pressures. In Colorado, very old Precambrian rocks cracked and faulted, and in many areas molten rock flowed up into these fractures. If the conditions were just right, the intrusions of molten rock formed veins of mineral-laden new rock. The search for and extraction of these minerals was the major factor in the development of Colorado.

It should be noted that the mountains of North America are not a single mountain range but rather a series of many ranges parallel to each other. There are about fifty mountain ranges in Colorado. The dictionary definition of "Range" is "(A) a series of things in a line, (B) a series of mountains." When you look at a Colorado map you will see that most of our ranges are oriented north and south. When the mountain men, trappers, traders, prospectors, and settlers came to Colorado, they were coming from the east. As they crossed the plains the mountains must have looked like an impassable wall. As they moved closer, they could see high ridges, valleys, peaks with differing heights, and gulches with rivers and streams. They found passes that made entering and crossing the mountains easier and safer. This book's definition of a pass is "a crossable low point on a mountain ridge or range that divides two river or stream drainages."

The purpose of this book is to provide the history of ninety-two passes that were built for and used regularly by wheeled vehicles: the freight wagons pulled by mules, the covered wagons bringing settlers pulled by oxen, the handcarts used by the miners, and the railroads. The book will explore why the passes were built, who built them, and how they were used.

As you read about these passes, think about the people who built them and the hardships they endured to achieve their goals. They were built in the post Civil War era. The armies of the North and the South were disbanding, leaving thousands of ex-soldiers to wander the country trying to find work. They wanted to start a new life away from the battlefields, destroyed towns and farms, and grieving families. The men

Acknowledgements

Many thanks to Kit Carson, John Dyer, Sidney Jocknick, and Otto Mears for giving us their autobiographies.

The historians who helped me write my "whodunnit" are, Paul Bonnifield, Christine Bradley, Nancy Christofferson, Leroy R. and Ann Hafen, Ed and Gloria Helmuth, Lee Kerrison, Donald W. Koch, Charles S. Marsh, James McTighe, Carolyn Newman, Jan Pettit, Len Shoemaker, Marshall Sprague, Duane Vandenbusche, and Lou Wyman.

Many librarians in Colorado provided written history for this book. I begin with thanking my Glenwood Springs Librarians: Pat Conway, Darla Baumli, Toni Carsten, and Karen Murphy. I thank Jackie Spuhler of the Eagle Public Library, the reserve staffs of the Colorado Springs Main Library, and of the new History Colorado Library in Denver.

My hearty thanks go to U.S. Forest employees Richard Doak, Leigh Ann Hunt, Bill Kight, and Laura Van Dusen.

Thanks also to friends who helped bring this book to you. They are Milt Cass, Joe Eaglesfether, John Horn, Patt Jones, the Ouray Historical Society, Joan Pinamont, Sandy Shimko, Cindy Williams, Laurel J. Williams and Bill and Pat Wolford.

TABLE OF CONTENTS

Tomichi Pass	148
Black Sage Pass	149
Monarch Pass	150
Poncha Pass	151
Marshall Pass	152
Hayden Pass	153
Town of St. Elmo	154
Towns of Romley and Hancock	155
Medano Pass	156
North La Veta Pass	158
Pass Creek Pass	159
Sangre De Cristo Pass	159
La Veta Pass	160
Cordova Pass	162
Cucharas Pass	163
La Manga Pass	164
Cumbres Pass	165
Raton Pass	166
Conclusion	169
Bibliography	171
Index	177

TABLE OF CONTENTS

Hoosier Pass 101
Kenosha Pass 102
Red Hill Pass 103
Mosquito Pass 103
Weston Pass 106
Trout Creek Pass 107
Currant Creek Pass 108
La Salle Pass 109
Wilkerson Pass 110

San Juan Regional Map 111
Owl Creek Pass 112
Town of Ouray 113
Dallas Divide 114
Black Bear Pass 115
Town of Telluride 117
Imogene Pass 118
Lizard Head Pass 119
Ophir Pass 120
Red Mountain Pass 123
Molas Pass 126
Coal Bank Pass 126
Engineer Pass 127
Cinnamon Pass 129
Town of Silverton 130
Stony Pass 131
Slumgullion Pass 132
Spring Creek Pass 134
Town of Lake City 135
Los Pinos Pass 136
Wolf Creek Pass 137
Elwood Pass 137
North Cochetopa Pass 139
Cochetopa Pass 139

Continental Divide–Southern Region Map 141
Palmer Divide 142
Ute Pass on Hwy. 24 143
Altman's Pass 144
Williams Pass 145
Hancock Pass 147

TABLE OF CONTENTS

    Milner Pass 51
    Fall River Pass 52
    Rollins Pass 53
    Berthoud Pass 55
    Golden Gate Pass 56
    Jones Pass 57
    Ute Pass (Off Hwy, 9, on Hwy. 132) 58

Gunnison Country Regional Map 59
    Blue Mesa Summit 60
    Cerro Summit 61
    Cottonwood Pass (South of Gypsum) 62
    Hagerman Pass 62
    Independence Pass 64
    McClure Pass 66
    Schofield Pass 68
    Pearl Pass 70
    Taylor Pass 71
    Kebler Pass 73
    Ohio Pass 75
    Tincup Pass 77
    Towns of Virginia City and Tincup 78
    Cumberland Pass 79
    Waunita Pass 80
    Town of Pitkin 81

Continental Divide-Central Regional Map . . . 82
    Vail Pass 83
    Shrine Pass 83
    Fremont Pass 84
    Tennessee Pass 86
    Town of Leadville 87
    Cottonwood Pass (On the Continental Divide) . . . 88
    Loveland Pass 90
    Argentine Pass 91
    Guanella Pass 94
    Town of Georgetown 96
    Webster Pass 97
    Georgia Pass 98
    Boreas Pass 99
    Town of Breckenridge 100

Table of Contents

Acknowledgements 1
Introduction 3

PART 1 5
Chapter 1: Mountains, Rivers & Plateaus 6
Chapter 2: Indians 9
Chapter 3: Explorers 12
Chapter 4: The Surveyors 14
Chapter 5: The Pathfinder, Otto Mears 15
Chapter 6: Colorado's Mineral Belt 18
Chapter 7: The First Railroads 23
    Denver and Rio Grande 23
    Colorado Central 25
    Denver, South Park and Pacific 25
    Colorado Midland 28
    Silverton Railroad 30
    Silverton Northern 30
    Silverton, Gladstone and Northerly 30
    Rio Grande Southern 31
    The Moffat Tunnel 32
    Dotsero Cut-off 34

PART 2 35
Chapter 8: The Historic Passes & Towns 36
    Map of the Regional Locations 36

    Northwest Colorado Regional Map 37
        Baxter Pass 38
        Douglas Pass 39
        Yellow Jacket Pass 41
        Dunckley Pass 43
        Buffalo Pass 43
        Rabbit Ears Pass 44
        Muddy Pass 45
        Gore Pass 46

    Continental Divide-Northern Regional Map 48
        Willow Creek Pass 49
        Cameron Pass 50
        La Poudre Pass 50

CHAPTER 1:
THE MOUNTAINS, RIVERS, PARKS AND PLATEAUS

The Ute Indians called them the "Shining Mountains." Lewis and Clark named them "The Rocky Mountains." The Rockies are the longest mountain barrier in the world. From the north, the ranges begin with the Alaska Range, and then continue on across Canada and the United States as the Rocky Mountains to end in the Sierra Madres in Mexico.

The Continental Divide is a meandering high crest in the Rockies that determines the direction of the waters flowing out of the mountains. From its top, the rivers that flow east include the South Platte, North Platte, Rio Grande, Arkansas, and Missouri which carry water to the Gulf of Mexico and the Atlantic Ocean. From the top of the Divide the water flows west in the rivers named Colorado, White, Yampa, Eagle, Gunnison, San Juan, and Uncompahgre water heads to the Gulf of California and the Pacific Ocean.

Colorado's highest mountain is Mount Elbert rising to an elevation of 14,433 feet. It is the third highest mountain in the United States. If a mountain has only one high point, it is called a "peak." If the mountain has more than one high point, it is called a "mountain." Fifty-three fourteeners, mountains over 14,000 feet in elevation, are located in Colorado with Gray's Peak and Torrey's Peak the only fourteeners on the Continental Divide.

The first name used for today's Colorado River was "Grand;" it was given by the French trappers. The name of "Rio Colorado" (river red) was first used for a tributary of the Colorado River by the Spanish explorer Juan de Onate in the early 1600s. When the Colorado Territory was organized in 1861, the U.S. Congress chose to name the territory and later the state, Colorado. "Colorado" is Spanish for red and ruddy.

The French word "parc" is translated as "a game preserve." Colorado has four intermontane parks, broad and flat basins that were created at the same time as the mountains. They are named North, Middle, and South Park and the San Luis Valley.

The Ute Indians were the first to call North Park the "Bullpen" because of the large herds of buffalo and elk living there. North Park extends into Wyoming. The Park Range Mountains on the Continental Divide are the west boundary of North Park, with the Rawahs and Medicine Bow Ranges on the east side. The Park's southern boundary, which divides it from Middle Park, is the Rabbit Ears Range. The North Platte River begins southwest of today's town of Walden and flows north into Wyoming. The elevation of North Park is about 8,800 feet above sea level. Muddy Pass and Willow Creek Pass provide crossings from North Park over the Continental Divide to Middle Park.

THE MOUNTAINS, RIVERS, PARKS AND PLATEAUS

Middle Park is the smallest of the montane parks with the average elevation of 8,000 feet. One of the Colorado River's headwaters begins in Middle Park. The Park is also the home of Rocky Mountain National Park.

Starting on the south side of the Continental Divide, near La Poudre Pass, the Colorado River starts flowing southwest. Over many years the river has carved many beautiful canyons on its journey to the Pacific Ocean. It receives water from 242,000 square miles in seven western states. It is our country's sixth longest river, receiving about seventy percent of its water from normal mountain snowmelt.

South Park has the highest elevation of the three parks at about 10,000 feet. It is the headwaters of the South Platte River, ("Platte" is French for "flat or shallow.") The Park's eastern boundary is the Tarryall and Rampart Ranges, the west boundary is the Mosquito Range, the southwest boundary is the Buffalo Peaks, while the south boundary consists of unnamed volcanic hills. The north boundary of the Park is the Ten Mile Range and the Mt. Evans sector of the Front Range. A low ridge named Red Hill runs north to south down the middle of the Park. Two early historic railroads crossed the Park. They were named the Colorado Midland and the Denver, South Park and Pacific.

The San Luis Valley starts at Poncha Pass on the north and in Colorado ends at the New Mexican border. The valley is fifty miles at its widest and about 100 miles long. The valley is bordered on the east by the Sangre de Cristo Mountains and Culebra Range, on the north by the La Garitas and on the west by the San Juan Mountains. Much of the valley receives little moisture and without irrigation, farming and ranching would not be possible.

The San Luis Valley is the home of the Great Sand Dunes National Park. They are the tallest sand dunes in North America and are located on the western side of the Sangre de Cristo Mountains. Sand blowing off of the San Juan Mountains to the west and dry lake beds in the valley hit the Sangre de Cristo Peaks and drop to form the dunes. The dunes are about six miles west to east, seven miles north to south, and up to 750 feet tall.

The uplifted plateaus are the unique geological feature of the Rocky Mountain's Western Slope. The word "plateau" is French meaning "flat." The plateaus were carved into canyons by the Colorado River and its many tributaries. The northern plateau is named the "White River," a fifty mile-long uplift bordered on the north by the White River and on the south by the Colorado River.

In October of 1891, President Benjamin Harrison signed a bill setting aside public lands for the public good. The areas were first called Forest Reserves. Yellowstone was the first Reserve, White River was the second. In 1919, a landscape architect named Arthur H. Carhart was sent to lay out home sites around Trappers Lake. The beauty of the area convinced him to work for wilderness preservation. The National Forest System was formed, and the Wilderness Act of 1964 became the law to protect and preserve our forests.

The White River Plateau is also the home of the Flattop Mountains. They look like some giant cut off their tops with his bowie knife. Their names include Trappers, Dome, Flattop, Shingle, Sheep, Shadow Turret, Marvine, and Little Marvine.

THE MOUNTAINS, RIVERS, PARKS AND PLATEAUS

Other plateaus in Colorado include the "Uncompahgre" northwest of the San Juans, the "Grand Mesa," the "Roan" above Anvil Points, and the "Book" above the Book Cliffs. The western edge of the Colorado Plateau is next to the lower Utah border.

CHAPTER 2: THE INDIANS

Before the introduction of the European culture into today's United States, the residents of our country were the people we call the American Indian. In 1492 Columbus named them "Los Indios" because he thought he had landed in the Orient. The Indians of Colorado, Utah, and Northern New Mexico were the Utes. Their ancestors were the Paleo-Indians, hunting people of Asian origin. Clovis and Folsom weapon points, found in the remains of mammoths, date Indian presence to as long ago as about 10,000 B.C. The Anasazi and other Pueblo Dwellers were living in the Four Corners Area of Colorado until about 1100 A.D. The Fremont Indians lived in Northwest Colorado until 1300 A.D. They left us scenes of their daily lives in "Rock Art," called pictographs and petroglyphs.

The Utes were living in Northern Colorado in 1776 when the "Fathers" Dominguez and Escalante, came up from Santa Fe looking for a route to the California Missions. In the 1820s to the 1830s the Utes helped the early beaver trappers and fur traders.

On his second voyage to America, Columbus by the order of the King of Spain, brought the first horses to America. In time the Spaniards brought them into New Mexico. It is reported that the Ute Indians were among the first to acquire the "Magic Dogs," their name for the horse in 1640. The horse enabled them to travel farther and faster and to carry more food and supplies. The horses and the travois they pulled made the game trails the Utes used much wider. The Utes hunted bison, deer, and elk for their meat as well as turkey, grouse, and other birds. They built wickiups for temporary housing made of willows and covered them with juniper bark and grasses. Their winter lodges used poles for strength which they covered with bison hides, with a firepit in the middle for cooking and warmth.

By the early 1800s the Ute Indians had migrated from Utah into Western Colorado and all the way to the Continental Divide of the Rocky Mountains. Before they had horses, they used dogs to pull travois loaded with leather packsaddles. When loaded, the dogs were tied together in a train.

Work roles for the Utes were gender based. The women were responsible for the gathering of roots and grains for cooking the daily meals, for making the clothing, for the moving and setting up of the teepees, and for caring of the young children. The men were responsible for training and tending the horses, for the making of weapons, and for the hunting and killing of the wild game. The women had the job of butchering the game and preparing the hides.

There were seven families or bands in the Ute Nation. The four Northern Bands were the Uncompahgre, Grand River, Yampa/White River and Uintah. The Southern Bands were called the Moache, Capote, and Weeminuche. Each band had its own leadership. The band chief was the principal chief who decided when and where to move for food, and he was the leader of the Council of Chiefs. The War Chief planned

THE INDIANS

the attacks and the defense of the band and would lead the warriors into battle. The Hunting Chief would lead the band's hunters to accomplish the killing of bison, elk, deer, and antelope for meat. The Council of Chiefs and sub-Chiefs would make final decisions for the band. The leaders were chosen for their moral power, wisdom, and spiritual strength.

Gradually one man emerged who had natural gifts for the leadership of the Ute Nation. Ouray was born to a Ute mother and an Apache father in the Uncompahgre Band in 1833. Ouray was trained as a shepherd. Early on he earned a winning reputation among his band for his fighting abilities against the Lakota Sioux and Kiowa. He was chosen to be the spokesman for the Ute Nation by his people and by the United States Government. In 1872 Ouray and his wife Chipeta and their interpreter Otto Mears traveled to Washington to meet with President Ulysses Grant to discuss new treaties. The Indians promised to move out of four million acres of land for which the tribe would receive an annual payment of $25,000.

The first Indian agency of the U.S. Government was established in New Mexico to distribute food and supplies to the Indians in return for relinquishing their lands. The agents were appointed to do the job of dealing with hungry and unhappy homeless Indians. In 1875 the Los Piños Indian Agency, located about twelve miles west of Cochetopa Pass, was ordered to be moved west to the much lower Uncompahgre River. The Utes were moved to today's town of Colona, south of today's Montrose.

In the spring of 1878, a new agent named Nathan Meeker was assigned to the White River Agency for the Northern Utes. He insisted on farming and Christianity as a new way of life for the Utes, which most of them strongly rejected. When Meeker insisted that they plow up the meadow that they were using as a horseracing track, one of the Indian leaders told Meeker to leave the agency. Other Utes fired warning shots at the farmhands when they started the plowing. Meeker sent a messenger to the Army at Rawlins, Wyoming, explaining what was happening at the agency. Two sub-chiefs of the Utes, Douglas and Jack, were the leaders of the uprising that Meeker started by trying to civilize the tribe too quickly. The Army sent Major Thomas T. Thornburgh with two companies of infantry, cavalry, soldiers, and a wagon train. They arrived at the area where the wagon road crossed Milk Creek about twenty-five miles north of the White River Agency. It was here that Thornburgh's men were ambushed, the Major and twelve of his men were killed, and forty-three men were wounded.

Word was sent back to Rawlins for help. Captain Dodge's Command of forty "Buffalo Soldiers" rode in from Middle Park to support the Thornburgh men who were wounded in the battle. General Merritt's Command arrived on Sunday from Rawlins to help put an end to the violence and soldier deaths. The Indians disappeared soon after his arrival. General Merritt moved south to the agency on the White River and found Meeker and his white employees dead. The raiding of the agency was the work of Quinkent, now known to us as Douglas, who was a sub-chief, and sub-chiefs Colorow and Jack, who had stayed at the agency during the battle at Milk Creek. It is highly probable that they took the lead in killing Meeker and his staff. Meeker's wife and two other women and a baby were taken captives. When Ouray heard about this, he sent General Charles Adams to secure their release, which he did, finding them moderately well treated. Ouray and Chipeta made one final trip to Washington to sign

THE INDIANS

a treaty by which the White River Utes would be relocated to the Uintah Reservation in Utah.

On a trip to the Southern Ute Agency, Ouray died and was buried near Ignacio on August 24, 1880. A short time later the Uncompahgre, Yampah, White River, and Grand River Utes were forced out of Colorado to the Uintah Reservation in Eastern Utah. Ouray's wife Chipeta died on the Uintah Reservation in 1924.

The Southern Ute reservation was established in southwestern Colorado, a 15 by 100 mile strip of land, for the Southern Utes. In 1895 the U.S. Government's Hunter Act repealed all of the 1888 treaties and established permanent reservations. In 1906 an agreement was reached to trade the Utes' more land on the Utah border for the Mesa Verde Cliff Dwellings. In 1924 all American Indians were allowed to become United States Citizens. During the 1930s, the Ute Bands on the Uintah Reservation organized a business council with elected representatives from each band and incorporated as the Northern Ute Tribe. In 1936 the Southern Utes adopted a constitution and tribal council. In 1938 a U.S. Government Restoration Act returned land to the Southern Utes. Land was also returned to the Ute Mountain Indians after they adopted a constitution in 1940.

Today the Uncompahgre, Yampa, White River, and Grand River Bands live on the Uintah-Ouray Reservation with headquarters at Fort Duchesne, Utah. The Moache and Capote Bands are the Southern Utes with their headquarters at Ignacio, Colorado. The Weeminuche Band is now called the "Ute Mountain Utes" and live on their reservation near Towaoc, Colorado.

CHAPTER 3:
THE EXPLORERS

The first European-Americans to live and work in Colorado came hunting for beaver pelts. Beaver hats were in demand for the wealthy men and women back East and in Europe. Fur companies, such as the Hudson Bay Company and the American Fur Company, hired young men to trap beaver. The fur company transported the pelts, which could sell for up to $30 each, to the largest cities on the East Coast.

General William H. Ashley and Major Andrew Henry of Missouri formed the Rocky Mountain Fur Trade Company in 1823. Their destination for trapping was Colorado. Among the young men hired were Jedidiah S. Smith, a bible toting and quoting New Yorker; James Bridger, a natural-born geographer; Thomas Fitzpatrick; William Sublette; and Captain John Weber. At first they trapped in south central Wyoming. The owners of the fur company quickly made their fortune and returned to Missouri.

Some of the trappers stayed to go out on their own in Colorado to trap and trade beaver pelts. They also became guides for those who followed them. They included Kit Carson, Old Bill Williams, Hugh Glass, James Beckworth, Jeremiah Johnson, Cerain St. Vrain, and Thomas L. "Pegleg" Smith. When beaver hats went out of style in the 1830s, the fur trade faded and silk hats became the new fashion statement. Many of the trappers became guides for other hunters and for settlers.

In 1706, Captain Juan De Ulibarri led soldiers and settlers northward from Taos, New Mexico, along the Wet Mountains to the Arkansas River in search of invading Frenchmen and hostile Indians. They found evidence — a new French rifle — but did not encounter any opposition.

In July of 1776, two Franciscan priests left Santa Fe to find a trail that would connect Spanish New Mexico with Spanish California. Fathers Francisco Dominguez and Silvestre de Escalante led a small group of men north along the Dolores, San Miguel, and Uncompahgre Rivers to the Gunnison area. Their Captain Don Miera, an artist and engineer, drew the first surviving detailed map of today's Colorado. They also brought along a Ute Indian interpreter. Friendly Ute Indians kept heading the Fathers northwestward to show them the lakes of Grand Mesa and the deep canyons of the Colorado River. On September 6, 1776, they crossed the Colorado River close to De Beque Canyon and then followed Roan Creek up to the Roan Plateau. They followed the White River towards the Wasatch and Uinta Ranges in Utah, reaching Utah Lake near Salt Lake City. Winter stopped them cold! They turned south to escape the snow, arriving back in Santa Fe on January 2, 1777. This was the most important Spanish exploration because of Captain Miera's maps and Father Excalante's diary.

Once again, the hostile Comanche Indians became a problem in Colorado. Governor Juan Bautista de Anza left Santa Fe in August of 1779 with a force of 103 soldiers and 470 colonists. They reached the Comanche's camp on the Great Plains near today's Colorado Springs. Chief Cuerno Verde and 200 of his warriors were not in

THE EXPLORERS

camp, having gone south towards Taos. Anza's soldiers chased them, caught up with them, and defeated the Comanches.

In 1806, President Thomas Jefferson sent Lt. Zebulon Pike with about seventy-five men to explore Colorado. In November of 1806, his company entered Colorado and on November 15 sighted today's Pike's Peak. Pike and three soldiers attempted to climb the mountain but were stopped by a blizzard. Later the party entered South Park and crossed the Arkansas River. On returning home, they produced the first detailed reports and maps of southeastern Colorado. Pike rose to the rank of General of the Army but was killed during the War of 1812.

The War of 1812 interrupted exploration of the West until 1819, when Major Stephen H. Long and his party headed west. His party followed the South Platte River into Colorado, camping on the future site of Denver on July 5, 1820. Dr. Edwin James of the Long Party led two soldiers on the first recorded ascent of Pikes Peak.

In June of 1842, Lt. John Charles Fremont led his first expedition for the United States Army Corps of Topographical Engineers from St. Louis to map the Oregon Trail as far as South Pass in Wyoming. Part of his party followed the Oregon Trail up the North Platte, while Fremont and the others traveled up the South Platte looking for sites to build forts. He met up with the rest of the expedition at Fort Laramie in Wyoming. He and his men were back in St. Louis by mid-October of 1842.

By July 7, 1843, they were back at Cherry Creek near Denver. They traveled to North Park, then went south through Middle Park into South Park and home to St. Louis on August 6, 1844. In the summer of 1845, Fremont made his third trip into Colorado. He followed the Arkansas River up past Mt. Elbert to the site of Leadville. From Leadville he went north to discover what later would be called "Tennessee Pass." When he returned to St. Louis, Fremont and his wife Jessie published his reports and maps of Colorado. In the fall of 1848, retired Colonel Fremont, guided by "Old" Bill Williams, made his last trip into the San Luis Valley. A blinding blizzard grounded the expedition in December. Bad judgments were made by the leaders resulting in eleven men freezing to death. They finally found the upper Rio Grande River and followed it downstream to Taos, New Mexico.

In 1853, Captain John Gunnison led a Pacific Railroad survey west across the Continental Divide over Cochetopa Pass headed for Salt Lake City. Their goal was to find a route to Salt Lake going over Sangre De Christo Pass and Cochetopa Pass. In early August, they crossed Poncha Pass, then followed Poncha Creek west to what would later be called Marshall Pass. The next day at noon, on September 2, they crossed Cochetopa Pass and followed Cochetopa Creek north to enter the high valley of the Gunnison River. They fought their way around the Black Canyon of the Gunnison River to the Uncompahgre River, traveled north to today's Grand Junction, then west into Utah, arriving at Sevier Lake, Utah. A California-bound wagon train had camped in the Sevier Lake area, and in a skirmish with the Paiute Indians had killed the father of the tribe's chief. Gunnison's party was the next white men to reach Sevier Lake. On October 26, 1853, eight men died, including John Gunnison, from an attack by Paiute Indians. Lt. G. Beckwith led the survivors home and spoke against the proposed route for a railroad because of the rough terrain.

CHAPTER 4:
THE SURVEYORS

The policy of the Federal Government was to make its land accessible to potential settlers. In order to inventory it, they first had to survey it. The four great surveys of Colorado were led by John Wesley Powell, Clarence King, Lt. George Wheeler, and Ferdinand Hayden in the years 1868 through 1876.

Major John Wesley Powell, a one-armed Civil War veteran, led the first recorded ascent of Longs Peak in 1868. His most famous survey took place between 1869 and 1871 when he led a daredevil boat inspection of the Green and Colorado Rivers.

Clarence King's survey was commissioned for the Union Pacific Railroad to find a possible route through Nebraska and Wyoming. He also surveyed Northern Colorado for the same reason in 1867-1872.

Between 1871 and 1878, Lt. George Wheeler surveyed Southwestern Colorado and most of the American Southwest.

In 1873 the newly created United States Geological Survey sent Ferdinand V. Hayden to systematically map western Colorado from the mountaintops. His surveyors were the first to climb and name many Colorado peaks. The major result of their survey was the mapping of 69,000 square miles of the Colorado Rockies during the summers of 1873 to 1875. The team of the medical doctor turned geologist was divided into three groups. Each group of six to eight people included a topographer and his assistant, a geologist or two, packers, and a cook. Each man rode a mule. The packer led a packtrain of five to six mules carrying tents, food, cooking gear, and instruments. They had an odometer for measuring mileage and a barometer for measuring altitude. Their lead photographer was a young unknown man named William Henry Jackson.

Hayden began his team surveys in the Middle Park area. Later Hayden himself led a team into the Gunnison Country. His route brought him to Cement Creek and the present site of Crested Butte. From there he led them north across the Elk Mountains and reached the site of today's town of Gothic. He crossed Schofield Pass and followed Rock Creek, now called the Crystal River, to where it flows into the Roaring Fork and on down to the Colorado River. One of his parties was the first to report on the Mancos Canyon cliff dwellings in today's Mesa Verde National Park and the Mount of the Holy Cross. Hayden published "The Atlas of Colorado" in 1877, and his work remains the basis for all subsequent mapping. Hayden's maps as well as maps made by others became a way for any user to find the Colorado passes and the best ways to get to their destination.

CHAPTER 5:
THE PATHFINDER OF THE SAN JUANS: OTTO MEARS

When Otto Mears was eighty-six years old, he dictated some of his life story to his close friend Arthur Ridgway. This is a quote from that dictation.

I was born May 8, 1840 in Russia. My father died when I was one year old. When my mother died, an uncle took me into his family. When I was a little over nine, he sent me to England to another relative who in turn put me on a sailing vessel to America. Another vessel took me to Panama which we crossed by horseback, and then another boat to San Francisco. When the Civil War broke out I joined the First Regiment of California Volunteers in the spring of 1861. I fought the Navajos with Kit Carson until we were discharged in 1864. I moved to the old town of Conejos, Colorado, in the San Luis Valley and opened a general store there in 1865.

In 1870, Otto married Miss Mary Kampfshulte near Granite, Colorado. While living in Saguache, they were blessed by the birth of their daughters, Laura and Cora.

The Northern Utes were located on Los Piños Creek, just over Cochetopa Pass from Saguache. Otto obtained contracts to supply beef and merchandise to the Ute Indians at the Los Piños Indian Agency. Because of these contracts he became a great friend of the Ute Chief Ouray and by necessity mastered the Ute language.

The roads in the Colorado Territory were privately developed and owned. A charter to build a road could be obtained from the county for $5, and construction had to begin within ninety days. Neither the territory nor the county provided money for road building; the charter holder had to finance his own project. When the road was completed, the builder could collect toll charges, based upon the cost of building the road, for twenty years from the people who used it. At the end of twenty years, the road became the property of the State of Colorado or U.S. Government.

Mears' first toll road was chartered on November 8, 1870 for a wagon road to be built between the San Luis Valley and the Arkansas River Valley. The road was started at the town of Saguache on the northwest side of the San Luis Valley. He surveyed and built the road north through Villa Grove and over Poncha Pass three miles east of the Continental Divide. The road continued north through today's Poncha Springs to its terminus at Nathrop. This toll road was fifty miles long and is used today by U.S. Highway 285.

His second road had been charted and started by the Saguache and San Juan Toll Road Company to build a toll road from Saguache to Lake City. The company was failing because it was under-financed and lacked experienced leadership. Mears bought the stock and ownership of the charter. By August of 1874, he had raised the money to improve sections of the road already built and to finish the remaining sections of the road in the summer of 1875. The new road went west from Saguache over the Continental Divide on Los Piños Pass and on through the towns of Cochetopa, Powderhorn, and Barnum. From Barnum the road went south into Lake City. The importance of this road is that it connected the San Luis Valley to the Gunnison Country and the San Juan mining areas.

In 1875 the Ute Indians were ordered to move from the Los Piños Agency to the Uncompahgre Agency near today's Colona south of Montrose. A road was needed to carry supplies to the Utes. In 1875 and 1876 Mears built the Lake Fork and Ouray Toll Road to the Agency and beyond. He started at the town first named Barnum, then Allen and finally Gateview on the Lake Fork of the Gunnison River. From there he headed west to cross Blue Mesa Summit to today's town of Cimarron and over Cerro Summit to Montrose. The road was then built south to the agency and later to Ouray.

On August 20, 1883, Otto Mears incorporated the Ouray and Canyon Creek Toll Road Company, and had the road located and surveyed. Construction began on the first part of the road out of Ouray and it was completed by the end of September. The rest of the road was built into the Sneffels Mining District and the Camp Bird area; it was completed in the summer of 1884.

The major discovery of rich ore in the Yankee Girl Mine on Red Mountain in August of 1882 convinced the Ouray County Commissioners that they needed the services of Otto Mears. They wanted him to build them a road from Ouray up the Uncompahgre Canyon to the Red Mountain Mining District. In 1880 the county had incorporated the "Ouray and San Juan Wagon Road Company" to build the road, but after two attempts failed they gave up. The commissioners asked Mears to build the road, and on June 14, 1883, he said that he could and would build it. His cost would be ownership and control of the wagon road company. The canyon had two possible building sites, at the bottom next to the river, or high above the river in the quartzite cliffs. Mears' choice was to build a shelf road by using dynamite to remove rock from the top of the cliff. He lowered drillers on ropes to plant the dynamite, pulling them back to the top before lighting the fuses. He used this procedure to build this twelve-mile road up to Red Mountain Pass, completing it in September of 1883.

On June 8, 1884 the Silverton Town Council and Otto Mears signed a contract for Mears to build a road from Red Mountain Pass south to Silverton. Construction started on July 8, 1884, and it was completed on November 21, 1884. Mears considered the Silverton to Ouray road his greatest accomplishment, calling it the Rainbow Route.

When he stopped building toll roads in 1886, Mears had built a total of about 450 miles in southwestern Colorado. He was indeed the Pathfinder of the San Juans — a premier road contractor.

Along with his involvement in Indian affairs and road building, Mears was active in politics. In 1884 he was elected the representative to the State Legislature from Saguache County. During his service as representative, he was the chairman of the Committee on Counties and County Lines. He helped organize Montrose, Delta, and Mesa Counties.

In 1888 the State Assembly authorized the erection of the Colorado State Capitol. Otto Mears was one of the five men appointed to the Board of Capitol Managers to supervise the building of the capitol. The cornerstone was laid on July 4, 1890. The first offices were occupied in 1894. Mears served on the Board of Capitol Managers until he resigned on April 27, 1920.

The Mears family made their final home in Pasadena, California. Mary died on August 7, 1924 and Otto died at the age of ninety-one on June 24, 1931. According to the Mears' wishes, their ashes were scattered on Engineer Mountain above Animas Forks.

CHAPTER 6:
COLORADO'S MINERAL BELT

The Colorado Mineral Belt is the area that includes most of the mines, mining districts, and mining camps that have produced many millions of dollars worth of metallic and non-metallic minerals. As our map shows, the "comma-shaped" area starts above Boulder and heads southwesterly following the Continental Divide to Rico and Silverton. When George Jackson and John Gregory discovered gold in the Colorado Rockies, there were only four road passes over the Continental Divide — Muddy, Hoosier, Tennessee and Cochetopa.

The first method of extracting gold was using a pan or a sluice way to sift the sand and gravel of mountain streams for placer gold. In the spring of 1858, William Green Russell and John Beck met some "forty-niner" Georgian prospectors panning the waters of Cherry Creek in today's downtown Denver. They found only a trace of gold, not enough to keep them working, and they headed home.

On January 7, 1859, George A. Jackson found rich gold-bearing ore near today's Idaho Springs. He mined a rich vein of gold-bearing quartz above where Chicago Creek joins Clear Creek. On May 13, 1859, John Gregory discovered gold trapped in quartz in a gulch near the North Fork of Clear Creek. Today Gregory Gulch is located between Central City and Blackhawk. Although separated by mountains, Jackson's and Gregory's mines are only about five miles apart as the eagle flies.

The first Colorado mining district was organized on June 8, 1859, to establish legal claims and to enforce law and order in the mining camps. It was called the Nevada District and served the greater Central City area.

Prospectors George and David Griffith started panning for gold on the South Fork of Clear Creek in June of 1859. George discovered the "Griffith Lode" on the side of today's Griffith Mountain. He discovered rich ore of decomposed gold-bearing quartz. The Griffith Brothers were the first prospectors to discover silver in the Colorado Rockies. On August 1, 1859, they were looking for gold so they ignored the silver. The brothers built a cabin for housing, other men came to live and work, and they named the townsite "George's Town." They platted 640 acres for the town, formed a mining district, and built a tollroad from Central City to bring mining equipment for a mill.

The first mechanical method for extracting gold and silver from ore in Colorado was stamp milling. This method only removed about 30 to 40 percent of the metals. A Brown University chemistry professor named Nathan P. Hill studied smelters in England and Europe during 1865 and 1866. He was taught a system to remove metals called the "Swansea Process." It involved mixing copper sulfide ore with the gold and silver ore. The copper retained almost all of the metal present when the ore was removed. Hill moved to Black Hawk, Colorado, and built a smelter that used the Swansea Process. His company was called the Boston and Colorado Smelting Company.

COLORADO'S MINERAL BELT

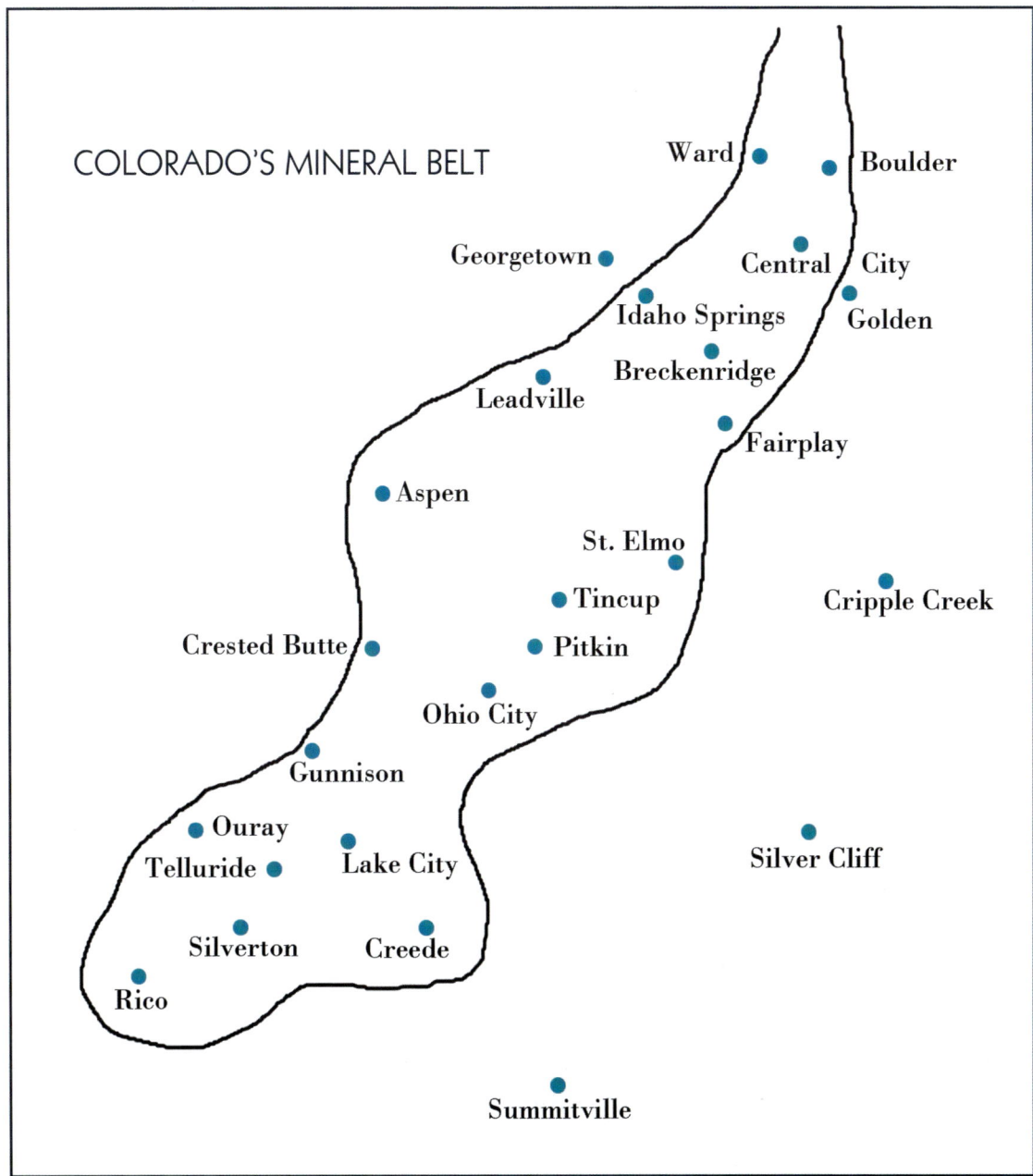

In Colorado, the first profitable mining of silver was the Belmont Lode, on Mt. McClellan near Georgetown in 1864 and the Caribou Lode, five and one-half miles northwest of Nederland in 1870. On September 14, 1864, James Huff, R.W. Steele, and Robert Taylor discovered silver-bearing ore at the headwaters of Leavenworth Creek. Huff also discovered a rich lode out-cropping on McClellan Mountain and helped organize the Argentine (the Latin word for silver) Mining District.

From the Georgetown and Silver Plume area, prospectors could cross Argentine Pass on the Continental Divide to work in Montezuma Basin and the Snake River Valley on the west side of the Divide. The first placer gold discovered in South Park was in Tarryall Creek in 1860. In 1869 a mining district was formed for the lode mines at

Tarryall, Alma, and Fairplay. The district included the mines on London Mountain on the eastern side of the Continental Divide.

The Mosquito Pass Road headed west out of Alma, through Park City to cross the Continental Divide on Mosquito Pass and continued down into today's Leadville. The first placer mining in the Upper Arkansas Valley was at Oro (Spanish for gold) City in California Gulch. The first lode mine, located high in California Gulch, was "The Printer Boy." In 1876, Alvinus Wood and William Stevens were the first prospectors to see that the black sands they were mining held silver and lead. In 1877, settlers chose the name of Leadville for their town. The town quickly grew to become Colorado's second largest city. The rich silver mines and the arrival of the railroads helped Colorado's highest city to grow. The narrow gauge Denver and Rio Grande arrived in 1880; the narrow gauge Denver, South Park, and Pacific in 1884; and the standard gauge Colorado Midland in 1887.

Following the Leadville Mining District's success, the prospectors crossed the Continental Divide using Hunter's Pass, today's Independence Pass. Two miles down the west side of the Divide, silver was discovered on July 4, 1880. The new mining camp was named Independence. The continued search for gold went downstream along the Roaring Fork River to Ute City. In 1880, B. Clark Wheeler suggested the name "Aspen" for the town because of the large aspen groves. Aspen's Smuggler Mine produced the largest native silver nugget ever mined, which weighed 1,840 pounds.

In 1880, H.B. Gillespie bought the charter to build a tollroad from Aspen into the Taylor River Valley, today's Gunnison County. He constructed the road south to Ashcroft and over a divide using today's Taylor Pass to the headwaters of the presently named Taylor River. This brought his road to the mining town of Tincup. From Tincup, a road traveled northeast to cross the Continental Divide on Cottonwood Pass and ended in Buena Vista. A second road out of Tincup crossed the Divide on Tincup Pass and ended in St. Elmo. A third road headed south over Cumberland Pass to the towns of Pitkin, Ohio City, and Parlin and on west to the town of Gunnison.

The mining towns on the west side of Gunnison County were called Marble, Crystal City, Schofield, Gothic, Crested Butte, Ruby, Irwin, Baldwin, Floresta, and Somerset. The passes connecting these towns were called Schofield, Pearl, Kebler, and Ohio.

The town of Cripple Creek is west of Colorado Springs about fifteen miles south east of Ute Pass. The Cripple Creek Gold District is on the west shoulder of Pikes Peak. It was the last and the biggest of Colorado's great gold camps. The United States Government had sent surveyor and geologist Ferdinand Hayden to survey and map Colorado in 1873. He reported that Cripple Creek drained an old volcano crater. He did not know that it was one of the world's greatest gold deposits. The first settlers to homestead in the area were William H. Womack and his brother Bob. In 1886, Bob staked a placer claim and in 1890 he filed a claim in Poverty Gulch for the "El Paso" (The Pass) Lode. The buried Cripple Creek volcano, at the elevation of 9500 feet, eventually produced 430 million dollars worth of gold. In 1915 "The Cresson Pipe," an intrusion in the volcano, delivered gold worth $1,200,000. It is estimated that Colorado produced 914 million dollars of gold between 1858 and 1958. Over one-half of this gold came from the Cripple Creek Mining District. Several major fires in

COLORADO'S MINERAL BELT

the business district, labor strikes, and flooding in most of the mines ended the Cripple Creek mining bonanza.

Gold and silver were first discovered by Spanish explorers in the San Juans. In the summer of 1860 American prospectors discovered gold in the San Juan Mountains. Mountain trapper and guide Charles Baker led prospectors from the Gunnison area south up the Lake Fork of the Gunnison River to today's Lake City. From there they went west over Cinnamon Pass into the headwaters of the Animas River. It was there that they discovered rich placer deposits of gold. The winter weather drove the men back to a warmer area. George W. Howard found a rich lode near Eureka in 1874. The town of Howardsville at the foot of Stony Pass is named for him. Other mines were discovered and developed at Animas Forks, Mineral Point, Gladstone, Eureka, and Silverton. The Eureka mines were the largest and longest producer in the headwaters of the Animas River.

When the search for silver and gold heated up in the San Juans, Otto Mears and Enos Hotchkiss bought a charter to build a tollroad from Saguache in the San Luis Valley to Lake City in the San Juans. Their road came west over Cochetopa Pass, then to the Lake Fork of the Gunnison River, and south to the present site of Lake City. Enos Hotchkiss was a surveyor and a prospector who discovered the first mine at Lake City. It was located at the north end of Lake San Cristobal and named "The Golden Fleece." Otto Mears also up graded the trail from Lake City to a rough wagon road over Cinnamon Pass. Merchants from Lake City built a toll road from Lake City over Engineer Pass into the Animas Forks Valley. Many mines and mills were built on Engineer Mountain at American Flats, and nearby at Mineral Point and Capital City.

In 1878 rich silver-bearing ore was found in three mines near Rico, southwest of Silverton. The white metal silver was the second most important element mined in Colorado.

A mining road out of Ouray went to the Tom Walsh mines, named the Lower and the Upper Camp Bird, and to Imogene Pass. A mining road out of Telluride led to the large Tomboy, Smuggler-Union and Liberty Bell Mines on the other side of Imogene Pass.

The Red Mountain Mining District covers the area next to today's U.S. Highway 550 between Ouray and Silverton. The towns were Albany, Ironton, Guston, Red Mountain Town, Congress, and Chattanooga.

The Yankee Girl Mine was discovered by John Robinson near Red Mountain Town in 1882. It was eventually a 1,200 foot vertical shaft of silver ore that became the richest and most famous silver mine in the United States. Just west of the Yankee Girl are the buildings and tailings of the Idarado Mine.

The town of Silverton is platted on a large open meadow called Baker's Park. In 1870 gold was discovered in Arrasta Gulch north of Silverton. The first productive mines here were "The Little Giant" and the "Mountaineer." There were many mines along the road north to the mining town of Gladstone providing "silver by the ton" to name Baker's Park's most famous town.

Charles Senter was prospecting on the western slope of Bartlett Mountain on Fremont Pass, north of Leadville. He found ore with veins of a dark material which he thought was graphite. He sent samples of the ore to the Colorado School of Mines at

COLORADO'S MINERAL BELT

Golden for their identification. In 1895 the staff of the school wrote that the mineral was molybdenum disulfide or molybdenite. The Climax Molybdenum Company was formed to recover and process the metal in 1916. During World War I, it was used as an alloy with steel to make armor plating and large gunbarrels. Since that time molybdenum is used to strengthen construction steels, tool and high-speed steels, stainless steels, for airplane engines, and for parts that must operate at high temperatures. Molybdenum was and is Colorado's biggest money-producing mineral.

Besides the obvious use for monetary purposes, gold is used in jewelry, in dentistry for fillings, crowns and bridges for dentures, eyeglass frames, and in photography as a gold toner. Gold is in the reflective layer on high end CD's and as a protective coating for satellites. It is also used for coatings and connecters in electronics.

Silver is used for coins, dental work, jewelry, "silverware" for eating, for coating solar reflectors, and for chalices and other religious uses.

Lead had been mined as a byproduct of the mining of silver in Georgetown and Breckenridge, but the largest production of lead-bearing ores began in Leadville. Together with other Lake County Mining Districts, Leadville produced one-third of Colorado's total lead production. Lead is used as an alloy in plumbing and construction supplies, gasoline, and batteries.

Zinc became important as a rust retardant in steel, as an alloy of copper in brass, and for die casting.

Copper is a by-product of other metal mining and is useful as an ornamental metal, plumbing, and in electrical wires.

Gold and silver miners often cursed "that damn black iron" which proved to be tungsten. It is metal used especially for electrical purposes and in hardening alloys.

The first discovery of pitchblende in the United States was at the Wood Mine of Central City in 1871. It is a mineral containing two radioactive metals, radium and uranium. Radium emits alpha particles and gamma rays to form radon which is used in luminous materials and in the treatment of cancer. Uranium 235 is used in nuclear power plants and atomic bombs.

Other elements and minerals mined in Colorado were vanadium, manganese, bismuth, cobalt, nickel, arsenic, antimony, and cadmium.

Colorado has an abundance of coal, sand, gravel, sulfur, petroleum, and natural gas. Colorado is second only to California in mineral variety and production. Colorado's passes were used to get to the mines and the mining towns.

CHAPTER 7: THE FIRST RAILROADS

Denver and Rio Grande Railroad

After the wagon roads, the next step was a railroad for fast and inexpensive transportation. On October 26, 1871, a brand new railroad engine with passenger cars left Denver headed south along the South Platte River. People watching noticed the name "Montezuma" painted on the side of the engine's cab, and the words "Denver and Rio Grande" on its tender. The words on the tender identify the location of the beginning and the proposed terminus of the railroad. Five hours later the narrow gauge train arrived at the new town of Colorado Springs. It was met by the railroad's owner and President General William J. Palmer and his board of directors. After a tour of the new townsite and a great meal, the passengers and the train returned to Denver.

In 1870 Palmer had obtained the property and financing for his railroad. The right of way came by a state charter of a strip of land 200 feet wide with twenty-acre tracts of land for depots and maintenance at ten-mile intervals. His financing came from W.P. Mellen, William Blackmore, Alexander C. Hunt, William A. Bell, and Robert H. Lamborn.

Palmer had proposed using the three-foot narrow gauge rails instead of the four-foot eight and one-half inch standard gauge width. The three-foot rails would mean cheaper construction costs and would allow thirty degree curves and four percent grades.

The D&RG was incorporated on October 27, 1870, with its headquarters in Denver. On December 1, 1870, the contract to build the railroad line was awarded to the North and South Construction Company of Philadelphia, Pennsylvania. The rails to Colorado Springs were to be completed by the end of 1871. On January 1, 1872, regular daily service started between Denver and Colorado Springs. The next section to be built was south to Pueblo, and the rails were ready for the first train on June 19, 1872. The locomotives were powered by steam produced by burning wood or coal.

The next section of rails continued south to Cuchara for its coal mines and to El Moro just east of Trinidad also for coal. Then the D&RG started a thirty-six-mile spur at Pueblo heading west to Cañon City, Florence, and the Coal Creek mines. The first train to use the new rails entered Cañon City on July 6, 1874.

The San Juan branch of the D&RG was started out of Cuchara in the spring of 1876. The rail line was headed for the San Luis Valley and beyond. They arrived at the Sangre de Cristo Mountains in July of 1876 and set up a railroad maintenance station and the town named La Veta. The rail builders used a muleshoe curve on the side of Dump Mountain with fourteen miles of three and four percent grades to reach the pass on the divide. Palmer built the first high altitude railroad crossing in North America. The contract for the rails to be laid to Fort Garland was approved in November of

THE FIRST RAILROADS

In 1882, the D&RG laid rails from Durango into Silverton to haul silver and gold ore from the San Juan Mountains. Today, the Durango and Silverton Narrow Gauge Railroad, using vintage equipment, operates over the same route hauling passengers.

1876 and completed during the summer of 1877. The rails to Alamosa went into service in June of 1878. In 1880 the D&RG headed south with its rails to Antonita and then west over Cumbres Pass, arriving at the town of Chama, New Mexico, on February 1, 1881. Turning west, they continued the rails to Durango, then north through the Animas River Canyon, arriving in Silverton in 1882.

In 1880 Palmer ordered his grading engineers and the construction crews to set rails west from Cañon City to Salida. From Salida they crossed the Continental Divide on Marshall Pass using Otto Mears' toll road which Palmer had purchased earlier. The first Denver and Rio Grande train whistled its arrival into the town of Gunnison on August 8, 1881. By the end of August of 1882, rails were built through Sapinero and the Black Canyon to Cimarron. In September the twenty-two mile section to Montrose was completed. Turning north, the rails were built to Delta in October. By Christmas of 1882, the track layers had completed this line to today's Grand Junction.

The northern branch of the D&RG left Cañon City for Salida on its way to the Leadville Mining District in the spring of 1879. From Salida they built tracks north in the Arkansas River Valley through the towns of Nathrop, Buena Vista, and Granite

THE FIRST RAILROADS

and arrived in Leadville in 1880. By the fall of 1881 the railroad had crossed Tennessee Pass to Red Cliff on the Eagle River.

The D&RG construction crews laid rails in the Eagle River Valley through Minturn to today's towns of Eagle and Gypsum. Continuing west, the rails entered the Colorado River Valley at Dotsero and followed the river through Glenwood Canyon. Two small tunnels, the Shoshone and Jackson, were bored in Glenwood Canyon. On October 4, 1887, the final rails were spiked down, and the first train arrived in Glenwood Springs on October 5. From there the rails went south in the Roaring Fork Valley to the town of Carbondale, arriving there on October 13. Their next railroad station was built at the confluence of the Frying Pan River with the Roaring Fork River. On October 13, the work train arrived in Aspen at about 4 p.m. The first passenger train whistled into Aspen at 4 p.m. on October 27, 1887.

Colorado Central Railroad

In 1861 one of the founders of Golden, Colorado had a dream of a transcontinental railway crossing the Rocky Mountains. The railroad would start in Golden and cross the Continental Divide near the headwaters of Clear Creek. The dreamer was William A. H. Loveland who incorporated the "Colorado Central Railroad" in 1872. It was a narrow gauge railroad, with three-foot wide rails, from Golden eastward into Denver. The next rails were laid to the west of Golden alongside the North Fork of Clear Creek to Blackhawk and Central City, the first gold rush mining towns. In 1876 and 1877 the rails were built up Clear Creek to Idaho Springs in June. On August 14, 1877 the rails were completed into Georgetown. Loveland's dream of his railroad ended for the lack of adequate financing. He sold the Colorado Central to Sidney Dillon and Jay Gould's Union Pacific.

Silver Plume was less than two miles west of Georgetown but it was almost 700 feet higher. The Georgetown Loop was designed by the Union Pacific as a spiral track that would cross over itself making three and one-half circles to gain the elevation to enter Silver Plume. The first train over the loop entered Silver Plume on March 10, 1884. The last rails of the Colorado Central were extended from Silver Plume to Graymont and ended in Bakerville.

The Denver, South Park and Pacific

Dr. John Evans was forty-eight years old when President Abraham Lincoln appointed him to be the Territorial Governor of Colorado. In 1863 Evans signed a treaty with the Ute Indians that moved them from the Los Piños Agency to a new agency on the Uncompahgre River near today's town of Colona. This opened up the San Luis Valley, the Arkansas River Valley, and the western Gunnison Country for prospectors, miners, town-builders, and settlers to live and work in peace.

The Denver, South Park and Pacific Railroad Company was organized in 1873. Ex-Governor John Evans was named as President of the Board of Directors for this new narrow gauge railroad. Seventeen miles of track were graded and laid west out of

THE FIRST RAILROADS

Denver. The railroad's locating engineer surveyed the rails to today's town of Bailey and the rails were laid in 1878. The rail laying continued west through Grant and up to Kenosha Pass and into South Park on May 19, 1879. They reached Como in late June of 1879.

In order to reach Leadville's silver boom, the Denver and South Park Railroad started laying rails north out of Como in 1880. They crossed the Continental Divide on Boreas Pass and followed Indiana Creek downstream into the town of Breckenridge. The rails were then laid north along the Blue River into Frisco. From Frisco the rails were built south along Ten Mile Creek to Wheeler Junction. Headed uphill the rails crossed the Continental Divide again, this time over Fremont Pass, and continuing south along the East Fork of the Arkansas River, rails were laid into Leadville.

Returning to his original goal, Evans' construction crew left Como to grade and lay rails south to Trout Creek Pass and down into the Arkansas River Valley. From today's Johnson Village the rails went south to today's Nathrop, then west up Chalk Creek to St. Elmo. The plan was to bore a tunnel for their rails through the Continental Divide.

The South Park Board of Directors chose to build their tunnel at the elevation of 11,496 feet underneath Altman's Trail. They hired James A. Evans to be their construction engineer and Robert A. Williams to be his assistant. Williams suggested building a supply road starting on the east side of the Continental Divide to move men and materials to the tunnel's east portal, and over the top of the Divide to the west portal. The supply road was built following the trappers' trail that "Old" Bill Williams used and it was named "The Denver, South Park and Pacific Alpine Toll Road." When the tunnel boring crew started, they assumed that they would be boring into solid granite. Instead of granite they bored into decomposed rock, loose rock and running water. They never did hit solid rock. The specifications for the 1,771 feet long tunnel included a height of seventeen feet and the width of twelve feet. The elevations of the tunnel were 11,496 feet at the east portal, 11,523 feet at the apex, and 11,521 feet at the west portal. With the altitude at the center of the tunnel being higher than at the portals, water would flow out of the tunnel.

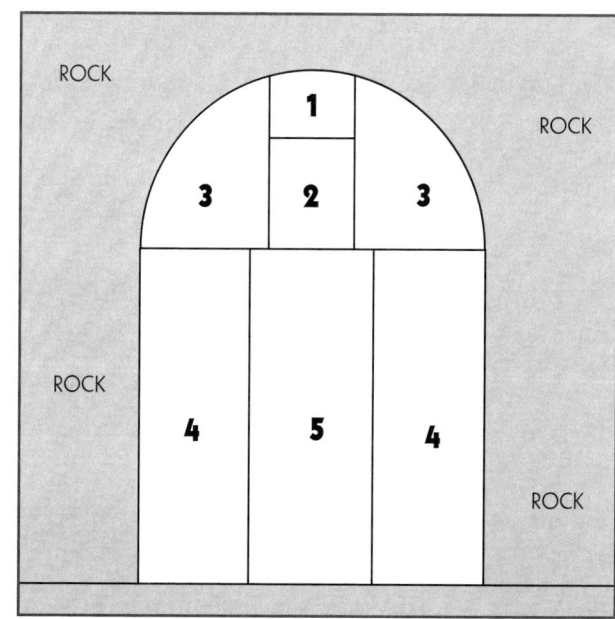

The boring system used to remove the rock from the tunnel was the German Center-Core Drilling System. A pilot bore was drilled at the apex of the tunnel to remove the rock from section one. Next, section two was removed down to the top sections four and five, creating a shelf for the crews to stand on to remove sections three. It also provided a base for timbering the ceiling to hold back the crumbled rock. Sections four were then removed down to the floor level leaving a

THE FIRST RAILROADS

The Palisade shelf-road was built by constructing dry-stacked rock walls and back filling then with rock to provide proper grade for the train rails leading to the Alpine Tunnel. This wall is 452 feet long and thirty-three feet high.

large core of rock in the center of the tunnel. All timbering would then be completed and section five would be removed.

The working conditions in the tunnel being built around the clock in the middle of the winter were terrible. Over 250 men were working the three shifts each day. The general laborers were paid $3.50 a day, while hard rock and explosives men received $5 a day. Contact between the portals and getting materials to the portals was difficult due to the high winds and deep snow.

On July 26, 1881, the two bores met and the tunnel was opened. The rotten rock at the ceiling and walls required additional redwood framing and covering to keep the tunnel dry. Heartwood redwood was chosen because of its hardness, slowness to ignite, and very slow rate of flame spread.

At the completion of the rock tunnel, rails were laid up Tunnel Gulch to the east portal in August of 1881. The rails were then laid through the tunnel to the west portal and Alpine Station. There they built a rock engine house that could hold six engines, a coal bin, wooden water tank, bunkhouse, section house, and a storage building. In April of 1882 the rails were being graded and laid downhill from the west portal.

The four-mile section of rails from the west portal to the Sherrod Loop is one of the greatest engineering achievements in the history of railroad building. In order to have a road for the rails across the vertical face of the Palisades, the engineers used the

THE FIRST RAILROADS

Williams Pass Wagon Road to build a shelf road. The contractors blasted out foundations above this wagon road to build a rock wall that would serve as the outer edge of their shelf road. After setting several layers of hand cut rock blocks, they filled loose stone behind the blocks and slowly built their shelf road up to the desired altitude. Sixteen times they dry-stacked rock walls and filled rock in behind to build their shelf road. The greatest example of their rock wall building is the great wall that is 452 feet long, thirty-three feet high and two feet thick, backfilled with smaller rocks to form the road. Another wall built on the Palisades to create the shelf road is 550 feet long and six feet high.

After crossing the Palisades the rails were laid to the Sherrod Curve. Today we would call it a hairpin curve. Directly below the Palisades a work camp was built to house the rock wall stone cutters and it was named Woodstock. The camp had a restaurant, general store, saloon, boardinghouse, telegraph office, water tank, coal shed, and a 500 foot rail siding. In March, 1884, an avalanche roared down the west-facing slope of Mt. Chapman and buried Woodstock, killing thirteen people and leaving many people injured.

In July, 1882, the South Park rails were laid into Pitkin and in August to Ohio City and Parlin. The final twelve miles into Gunnison were constructed, and the first South Park train whistled into Gunnison on September 8, 1882. The Alpine Tunnel was the first railroad tunnel ever built under the Continental Divide.

The Colorado Midland

James John Hagerman was a Milwaukee, Wisconsin, Iron Master who became wealthy working and investing in the Iron Ranges of Michigan's Upper Peninsula. He came to Colorado for treatment of tuberculosis at the Manitou Soda Springs near Colorado Springs. He invested in mines at Leadville and the Mollie Gibson Silver Mine at Aspen. The only railroad service for his mines at the time was Palmer's Denver and Rio Grande.

Hagerman decided to build his own railroad to compete with the Denver and Rio Grande. With the help of other investors, he incorporated the Colorado Midland Railroad on November 23, 1883. Its charter authorized it to build a standard-gauge railway from Colorado Springs westward to Leadville, Aspen, Glenwood Springs, and New Castle. The Colorado Midland Construction Company signed a contract on June 1, 1886 with the Colorado Midland Railway Company to build 250 miles of railway. Using his own money along with funds from his investors and a major loan from the Bank of England, he started to build his twenty million dollar railway. Hagerman and his board of directors decided to use standard gauge (4 feet 8 1/2 inch) wide rails for their railroad. It was the first standard gauge railroad to tunnel through the Continental Divide in North America. It was also chosen because the inter-continental railroads of the country used standard gauge.

Construction started west out of Colorado Springs on May 17, 1886, to cross the pass near today's town of Divide, later named "Ute Pass" to honor the Indian's trail.

THE FIRST RAILROADS

Many Indian tribes used this early trail to enter the mountains for hunting deer and elk and to cut trees to use for supports for their lodges. The railway followed Fountain Creek Valley upstream almost to the pass. It was necessary to build eight tunnels to complete the road for the rails up to Divide Pass. Another three tunnels were built through Eleven Mile Canyon to bring the railway into South Park. The rails crossed South Park by following the South Platte River to near Trout Creek Pass. The railway continued west along Trout Creek to its junction with the Arkansas River. The railway then headed north on the west side of the river through Buena Vista and into the towns of Granite and Leadville.

At Leadville the Colorado Midland hired a road contractor named Douglas to build a road west out of Leadville to the Continental Divide. He built the first wagon road in order to bring supplies and men for the construction of the first standard gauge railroad tunnel through the Continental Divide. He started the project by building twenty-five miles of rails to the base of the Divide.

I have chosen to write the history of building the two tunnels, the Hagerman and the Busk-Ivanhoe, through the Continental Divide in Chapter Eight, Gunnison Country Regional Section, page 62.

After exiting the Hagerman Tunnel on the west side of the Continental Divide, rails were laid west on the north side of Ivanhoe Lake. From the lake they followed Ivanhoe Creek. About three miles west of the lake, Ivanhoe Creek drops into a deep canyon. Above the canyon the rails were built on a narrow shelf road which a construction worker called "Hell Gate." A short tunnel, the last one on the Midland Railway headed west, was built on the shelf road.

Ivanhoe Creek joins the headwaters of the "Frying Pan River" near the deserted townsite of Nast. On the north side of the Frying Pan River the rails were laid across today's Sellar Meadow. A station was built with a depot, sand house, water tank, and bee-hive shaped charcoal ovens. Wood was used to make charcoal for fuel when coal was not available to make coke. The Sellar ovens also made charcoal to fuel the smelters of Leadville. Following the Frying Pan River downstream, the railway came to its confluence with the Roaring Fork River. During November of 1887 they built a station and called it "Aspen Junction." Today we call it Basalt. Their charcoal ovens provided fuel for Aspen's smelter.

From Aspen Junction the track layers headed southeast to Aspen, arriving at Maroon Creek on December 2, 1887. There they had to wait for the construction of the 600-foot steel bridge trestle to be completed across Maroon Creek. Reliable reports stated that the first train into Aspen arrived on February 4, 1888.

The Colorado Midland was sold on May 31, 1917 to the Cripple Creek tycoon Albert E. Carlton. On August 5, 1918, the federal courts ordered the financially crippled Colorado Midland Railroad to cease operations. By mid-October of 1921 the rails were removed and the railway was legally dissolved on May 21, 1922.

THE FIRST RAILROADS

The Silverton Railroad

After building hundreds of miles of mountain toll roads, Otto Mears, the "Pathfinder of the San Juans," started building his first railroad. The rails started in Silverton and were laid north across Red Mountain Pass into the Red Mountain Mining District. He hired Charles Gibbs to build his railroad. Mears' rails used the toll road he had constructed to the Red Mountains in 1883. The railway would use the three-foot-wide narrow gauge rails. In the summer of 1888, the grading was set and rails laid up the Mineral Creek Branch of the Animas River through the supply town of Chattanooga. They continued north around the Chattanooga Loop to the Red Mountain Summit. Mears named the station built at the top Sheriden, which at the elevation of 11,118 feet was the highest railroad station in the 4,000 square miles of the San Juans. From there he followed Red Mountain Creek past Red Mountain Town, Guston, Ironton, and Albany. He built a covered turntable in Corkscrew Gulch above Ironton and a station inside a wye at Red Mountain Town to get to the rich silver mines. Some of the big mines were named Carbon Lake, Congress, Genessee, Guston, Hudson, National Belle, Silver Crown, Silver Ledge and the richest and most famous of all silver mines, the Yankee Girl. The last mine to use the Silverton Railroad was the Silver Ledge on the Chattanooga Loop. The railroad was abandoned in the early 1920s.

The Silverton Northern

In 1893, Otto Mears started an extension of his "Silverton Railroad," headed north up the Animas River to Waldheim's Silver Lake Mill. In 1895 Mears and Fred Walsen incorporated the "Silverton Northern Railroad" to continue the rails to Howardsville. The next section to be graded and rails laid was the four miles to the Eureka mines. Other projects caused lengthy delays in the construction of this railroad, but in 1903 rails were extended into the Animas Forks Mining District. From there the railroad could serve the mines on Engineer Mountain, Mineral Point, Placer Gulch, and Animas Forks. The Silverton Northern was operational from 1893 to 1942.

The Silverton, Gladstone and Northerly

Gladstone was a small mining town at the headwaters of Cement Creek, six miles north of Silverton. Olaf Nelson discovered "The Gold King" lode in 1877 and sold it in 1893. In 1896 the new owners discovered a deeper and richer ore body in the Gold King. The mine's supervisor asked Otto Mears to build a railroad spur to Gladstone to move ore to the Silverton mills for processing. Mears turned them down. In 1899 the "Gold Kings" stockholders chartered and built their own railroad. They connected their narrow gauge railway to the Denver and Rio Grande Railroad in Silverton. The mine owners operated it until it was sold to Otto Mears' Silverton Northern in 1915 and went out of business in 1925.

The Rio Grande Southern

Otto Mears' Rio Grande Southern Railroad was incorporated on November 5, 1889. His railway started at Dallas Junction, later named Ridgway to honor R. M. Ridgway, the first superintendent of the Rio Grande Southern. Charles W. Gibbs was the chief locating engineer for the railway from Dallas Junction to Durango, Colorado. From Dallas Junction to Telluride, Gibbs used Mears' toll road route built in 1879. The first pass crossed by the R.G.S. was Dallas Divide. The rails continued west to Placerville, then south in the San Miguel River Valley to arrive at Vance Junction on November 16, 1890. From there a spur was built using a big loop to get into Telluride. Heading south from Vance Junction the railway was built on the west side of the San Miguel River Canyon until it crossed over the Howard Fork of the San Miguel River on the Butterfly Trestle. This Butterfly Bridge was so named because it crossed below the Butterfly Mine, and it was the beginning of the Ophir Loop.

The construction crew continued laying rails on trestles and shelf roads on the side of Yellow Mountain to a twenty-four degree "hairpin" curve using a 3¼ percent grade rise. After the loop the high line rails headed west to the Lake Fork of the San Miguel River and climbed south to Trout Lake and crossed Lizard Head Pass. The rails reached the rich silver ore of Rico's two best mines named "Enterprise" and the "Black Hawk." The rails continued south and were completed into Dolores in November of 1891. The rails then headed east out of Dolores and arrived in Durango in December of 1891. On December 21, the first train ran the Ridgway to Durango 162-mile Rio Grande Southern Railway.

The United States Government's purchase price of silver that was set by the Sherman Silver Act of 1890 brought prosperity to the San Juan Country. The government promised to buy four to five million ounces of silver a month. As the mine's production increased, the price of silver dropped rapidly. President Cleveland asked Congress to repeal the Sherman Act, which it did on October 31, 1893, and it ended the purchase of silver by the government. This brought chaos to all of Colorado's silver mining districts.

The Rio Grande Southern enjoyed nineteen months of operation before it collapsed and went into bankruptcy. The railroad was bought and sold repeatedly for a number of years. In 1931 Forest White was the superintendent and Victor Miller was the court-appointed receiver for the bankruptcy of the RGS. They ended the use of passenger trains because of the high costs. Miller and White decided to build a smaller automotive substitute for continuing mail and passenger service on the RGS Railway. Jack Odenbaugh, a Dolores mechanic, bought a 1925 Buick touring car for $50, rebuilt the engine and the rear axle, and built a rear box with side boards for $800. Motor No. One went into service on June 17, 1931. It was operated by one man, it was fueled by gasoline, and it paid for itself in less than a month on its round trip from Ridgway to Dolores. Six more larger and stronger motors were built. Motors Three, Four, Five and

THE FIRST RAILROADS

This "galloping goose" is located at Ridgway's train museum.

Seven were converted to passenger use only. They used a school bus rear end adapted for rails and were powered by Pierce-Arrow engines. The engines often overheated at the high altitudes. In order to cool them, the motormen would open the two-part hood, and the air movement would make the hood flap like the wings of a goose. The Galloping Geese moved passengers in the San Juans until the fall of 1951. The rails were abandoned and removed by 1952.

The Moffat Tunnel

While in New York City on a fundraising trip to raise money for building his tunnel and completing his road, David Moffat died on March 18, 1911. With his death his dream of building his tunnel almost died, but some of Dave Moffat's friends worked hard to keep his dream alive. On April 1, 1922, Colorado's Governor Oliver Shoup proposed a state-wide funding bill to build the Moffat Tunnel and to finance it with the sale of bonds. The State Legislature approved the bill on April 29, and Moffat's dream of a main-line railroad going through the Rockies across Colorado was going to happen. The Moffat Tunnel was built under James Peak in 1922 to 1927. It was built at the elevation of 9,094 feet to eliminate the Rollins Pass Crossing. At that time it was the second longest railroad tunnel in the United States.

The tunnel contract was awarded to Hitchcock and Tinkler, a firm that had done a lot of work on the Moffat Road. The tunnel was to be built through the Continental Divide about two miles south of Rollins Pass. The pioneer bore method of building a small tunnel paralleling the larger railroad tunnel made it possible to blast cross-cut openings for working in several areas along the main tunnel. With the small tunnel being bored ahead of the large tunnel, the drillers would know what kinds of rock that they would soon encounter in the large tunnel. Construction camps with housing, recreation facilities, schools, hospitals, workshops, and maintenance buildings were built at the east and the west portals. The actual construction was by drilling, blasting, and mucking to enlarge the bore and setting the ceiling and wall timbers.

As there are many excellent books written about the daily work, progress, problems, and lives of the people who built the tunnel, we will skip to the end of the tunnel story.

On February 12, 1927, the two construction crews met and the tunnel was open. It was sixteen feet wide by twenty-four feet high and six plus miles long. The walls and ceiling were covered with California Redwood, steel plates, and poured concrete or gunite. The crossties, rails, and ballast arrived and the track layers installed the tunnel rails. On February 24, 1928, the first freight train went through from the west to the east. The grand opening celebration took place on February 26, 1928. The smaller tunnel was then used for carrying western slope water into Denver.

The east portal of the Moffat tunnel can be seen from the Rollins Pass road.

Moffat "Old Timers" have said that the tunnel took twenty-three days off the train's schedule and twenty-three miles off the length of the route. It also changed the maximum grade of the rails from four to two percent, and reduced the maximum elevation by 2,440 feet making it possible to double the length of the trains. The tunnel removed the cost in dollars and lives ruined that had been necessary in order to keep the "High Line" open during the long winter snows.

The Dotsero Cut-Off

David Moffat's dream of building a transcontinental railroad ended in Craig, Colorado. The Denver and Salt Lake Railroad was making plans to extend the Moffat Road to the west by constructing a forty-mile railway along the Colorado River from Bond to Dotsero. At Dotsero the railroad would connect with the Rio Grande Western's main line and continue west through Glenwood Canyon into Glenwood Springs. The rail laying began at Orestod near Bond and was completed in June of 1934. In April of 1947, the Denver and Salt Lake Railroad merged with the Denver and Rio Grande Western. Dotsero was named for the decimal point zero marked by the surveyor at the start of the connecting track. Orestod is Dotsero spelled backwards.

CHAPTER 8:
HISTORIC PASSES & TOWNS

The first explorers and settlers came into Colorado from the south and the east. To most of them the mountains looked like an impassible wall. By following the rivers and streams, they discovered low openings and crossings, which we call passes. In the following chapter you will find a brief history of ninety-two mountain passes that had a road across them for wheeled vehicles.

The western half of Colorado and part of the eastern side of the Continental Divide has been divided into six regions. A map of each region provides the names and relative locations of its passes. The highway numbers and town names will help locate a pass. Exact pass locations can be found in the "Colorado Atlas and Gazetteer." On each map north is at the top of the page.

MAP OF THE REGIONAL LOCATIONS

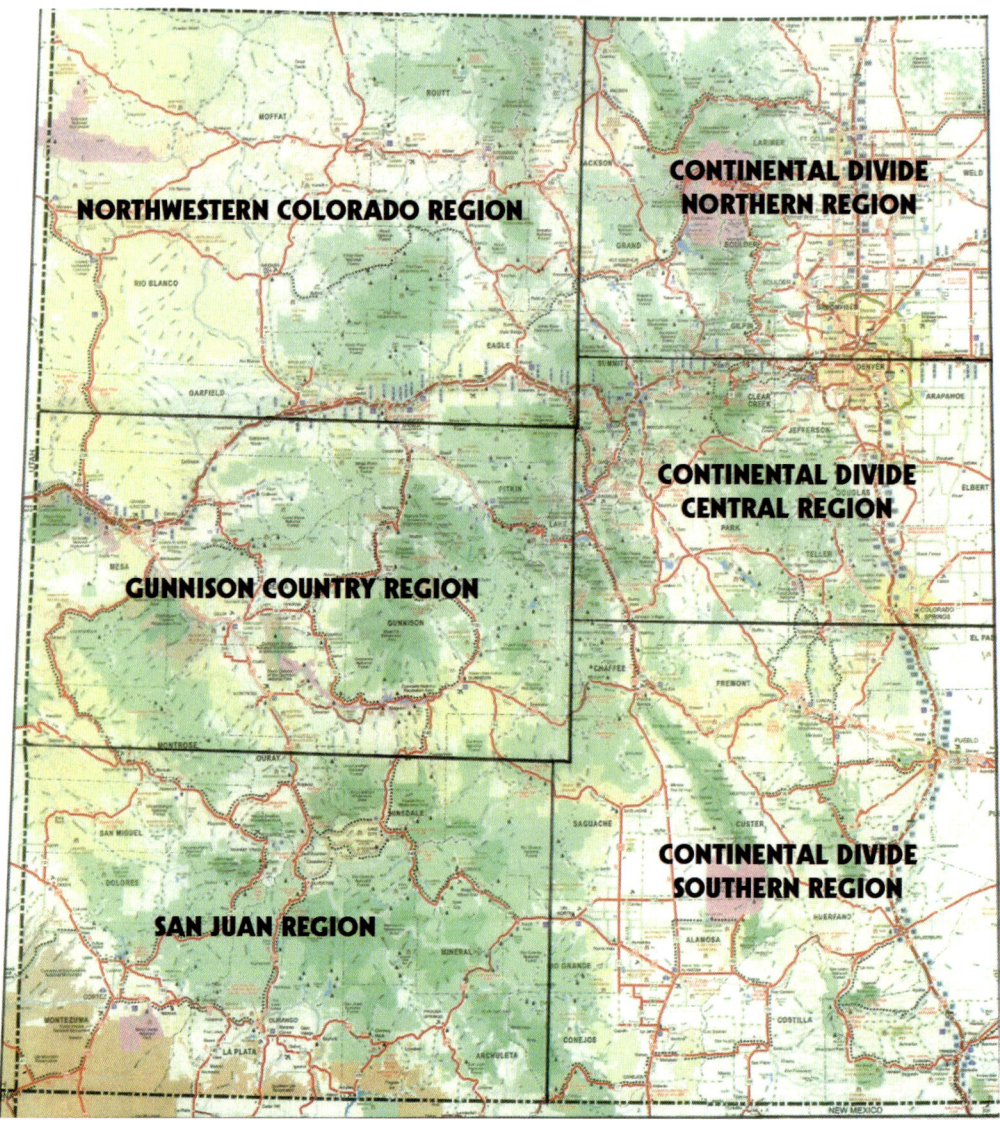

NORTHWEST COLORADO

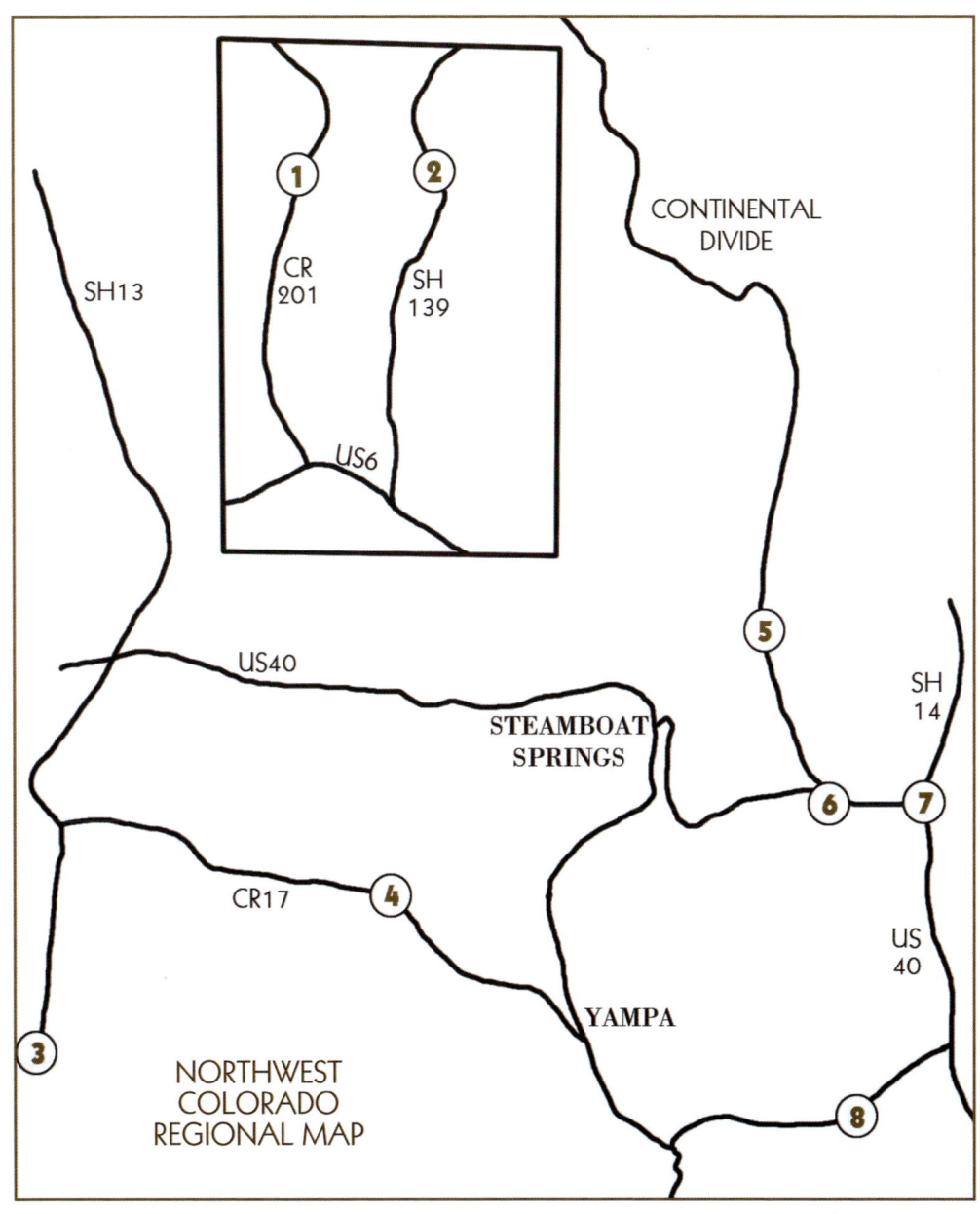

1   Baxter Pass
2   Douglas Pass
3   Yellow Jacket Pass
4   Dunckley Pass
5   Buffalo Pass
6   Rabbit Ears Pass
7   Muddy Pass
8   Gore Pass

NORTHWEST COLORADO

1
BAXTER PASS

GPS Location: N 39° 34' 55" W 108° 57' 09"
Elevation: 8,437 feet
First road over top: 1905
County: Garfield
On BLM Land

The early history of this low divide crossing indicates that it was an Indian trail. The Ute Indians and their ancestors could cross from the Colorado River Valley to the valleys of today's White and Green Rivers.

In 1885, on the Uintah Ute Reservation in eastern Utah, Samuel Gilson was shown samples of a mineral that was later named "gilsonite." It is a brittle, black asphaltic mineral looking like solid petroleum. When he left the reservation, he carried out an ore sack full of the mineral. Scientists could not determine if his ore was a mineral or organic. It was chewable and was eventually used as an additive in paint, insulating compounds, asphalt, printer's ink, and roofing material.

Samuel Gilson, C.O. Baxter, and John M. Mack, the president of the Barber Asphalt Company of St. Louis, Missouri, incorporated the Uintah Railroad to bring the gilsonite ore from the mines near Dragon, Utah. The railroad surveyors determined that the best route would be to connect their new railroad with the Denver and Rio Grande Western in Garfield County. They built north out of today's town of Mack into and over the Book Cliff Range on Baxter Pass and down to the Utah mines. Mack is twenty-two miles west of Grand Junction. They built a narrow gauge railway using three foot wide rails that could handle the grades of 7½ percent as well as many 66 degree curves.

Twenty-eight miles north of Mack they built a second company town named "Atchee" which was to be a maintenance center and provide housing for construction workers and operating crews. A regular narrow gauge engine brought the train to a turning wye at Atchee, where a "Shay" engine was used for the steep grades on the pass. After a few years, the company bought an "articulated locomotive" to handle the entire round trip. It worked so well that that they bought a second narrow gauge articulated locomotive. These two engines were the only ones sold for use in the United States. The dictionary definition of "articulated" is "an adjective—a vehicle having a hinge or pivot connection especially to allow negotiation of sharp turns."

The Uintah Railway completed its fifty-three miles of track over Baxter Pass in 1905. In 1939 the rail line was abandoned, and since then the gilsonite ore has been hauled by trucks.

NORTHWEST COLORADO

The Douglas Pass road as it approaches the summit from the north.

2
DOUGLAS PASS

GPS Location: N 39° 35' 51" W 108° 48' 11"
Elevation: 8,268 feet
First road over top: 1920s
County: Garfield
On BLM Land

The Douglas Pass Road is today's State Highway 139. It starts at Loma on U.S. Highway 6 and crosses the Roan Plateau to reach Douglas Pass on the Book Cliff Mountain Range. From the summit of the pass the road continues north to State Highway 64 at Rangely. The pass is named for the Northern Ute Chief Douglas. The pass road was built following an Ute Indian trail in the early 1920s.

The King of Spain appointed Juan Bautista de Anza to be the governor of his New Mexico Territory in the late 1870s. De Anza sent the first European explorers north from Santa Fe to find a trail that would connect the Santa Fe Catholic missions with the California missions. Fathers Dominguez and Excalante were led by a Ute Indian guide along the San Miguel River to cross the Uncompahgre Plateau to the Uncompahgre River Valley. They followed this river to its confluence with the Gunnison River and then went north to the Grand Mesa and the Colorado River. On September 8, they reached De Beque Canyon. Crossing the river they reached today's Douglas Pass and continued north through "Canyon Pintado."

Canyon Pintado is Spanish for "painted canyon." This canyon contains rock art sites "painted" by the Fremont and Ute Indians. Two methods were used to apply pictures to the rocks. A "petroglyph" was made by using a pointed stone to carve a design into the surface of rock walls. A "pictograph" was painted on the walls using pigments made from minerals and plants.

The Fremont people lived in parts of Utah, Idaho, Colorado, and Nevada between 600 and 1200 A.D. in small villages of pit houses dug into the ground. They were hunters, gatherers, and farmers and best known for their pottery, basketry, and rock art. At the Sun Dagger site in Canyon Pintado, they created holes in the rocks that lined up with the movement of the stars, solstices, and equinoxes. Their "Carrot Man" figures are like figures from the Fremont Culture in the Barrier Canyon of southern Utah.

The Ute Indians lived in the Douglas Creek Valley from about 1200 A.D. to the 1880s. They were hunters and gatherers, drawing scenes from their daily living on the rocks. One of the most interesting pictographs in Canyon Pintado is Kokopelli, who was a prominent figure in the cliff dwelling Anasazi mythology. Some Indians believed that he was "a hump-backed flute musician with flying dreadlocks" while others described "a trader wearing a back-pack who used his flute to call attention to his wares." His presence in the canyon indicates that the Anasazi could have traveled through Canyon Pintado.

In Canyon Pintado, many pictograph sites can be found off of the Douglas Pass road around Rangely. This example is located at the Sun Dagger Site.

NORTHWEST COLORADO

From the summit, the pass road can be seen descending to the Milk Creek battle site located at the foot of Thornburgh Mountain.

3
YELLOW JACKET PASS

GPS Location: N 40° 08' 54" W 107° 09' 25"
Elevation: 7,538 feet
First road over top: 1876
County: Rio Blanco
Public and private land

The name "Yellow Jacket" refers to wasp nests near this mild highway pass. This name is also used for a Western Colorado town and several high-country trails.

In the late 1850s, the U.S. Government built a stagecoach and freight wagon road from the Union Pacific Railway in Rawlins, Wyoming, to today's Meeker, Colorado. About sixteen miles north of Meeker this government road crossed Yellow Jacket Pass.

In 1861 Edward Berthoud and Jim Bridger were locating a stage coach route through the Rockies that would carry mail from Denver to California. They crossed the Continental Divide near today's Berthoud Pass, continuing west across Middle Park into the Yampa River Valley and north to today's town of Craig. From Craig they headed south and crossed Yellow Jacket Pass to today's Meeker.

NORTHWEST COLORADO

In the summer of 1873, Dr. F.V. Hayden's U.S. Topographical Surveyors left Middle Park over Tennessee Pass to map the Eagle River and locate the Mount of the Holy Cross. His team included the photographer William H. Jackson and the topographer Archibald Marvine. Jackson's photograph of the Mount of the Holy Cross became his most famous photo. The men continued north along wild game and Indian trails up into today's Flattops. They measured and mapped the mountains giving the name to this mesa and to its many lakes and streams. Traveling west, they arrived at the site of the White River Ute Indian Agency and the later town of Meeker. Continuing north, they crossed Yellow Jacket Pass on their way to Rawlins in Wyoming. On their maps published in 1876, this pass is identified and named as a wagon road.

In 1878 Nathan Meeker was appointed "Agent in Charge" of the White River Ute Indian Agency. He wanted to change the Indian life style from hunting and gathering to farming. The Ute men were horsemen and members of a warrior society, whose favorite sport was horse racing. Meeker foolishly decided to plow up the Indians' race track to more quickly reach his goal. When the Indians revolted, Meeker sent a scout to Rawlins for army protection.

Major Thomas Thornburgh led 150 soldiers of the Fifth Cavalry on the old military highway south into Colorado. His soldiers were met at Milk Creek by over 200 Ute Indians sent from the Indian Agency by Chief Quinkent, named Douglas by the U.S. Government and led by Nicaagat, also called Jack. Leaders from the Army and the Indians tried to defuse the situation until a shot was fired and the battle began on September 29, 1879. Thornburgh was shot and killed and Captain Payne assumed command. On the battle's third day, "Buffalo Soldiers" arrived to join the fight and on the sixth day General Merrit arrived from Rawlins with more cavalry and the Utes were defeated. Accounts vary among historians on the death counts. Fifteen soldiers were dead and thirty-five wounded. It was estimated thirty-seven Indians were killed. Historians now call this event "The Battle of Milk Creek."

At the same time, the White River Ute Indians committed "The Meeker Massacre" at the White River Agency, killing Nathan Meeker and his white employees. Meeker's wife Arvilla, daughter Josephine, and a Mrs. Price along with her two children were taken as hostages. Chief Douglas led the Indians from the agency to their ancestral hunting grounds on the Grand Mesa. Chief Ouray organized a "peace party" to find the Utes and secure the release of the hostages. General Charles Adams and Ute elders found the Utes on the Grand Mesa and returned the hostages to their families.

NORTHWEST COLORADO

4
DUNCKLEY PASS

GPS Location: N 40° 12' 06" W 107° 09' 31"
Elevation: 9,763 feet
First road over top: mid 1890s
County: Rio Blanco
Routt National Forest

This pass road was first used as a migration trail by the Ute Indians moving west from the Yampa River Valley to the White River Valley. The Dunckley Pass road crosses the southern end of today's Dunckley Flat Tops.

The Dunckley Family was the first to settle in this area. The brothers John, Thomas, Robert, George, and Richard homesteaded here in the mid-1890s. They had come to raise cattle and their families in the broad valleys on the eastern edge of the White River Plateau, and were responsible for the construction of the first freight road into this country. The wagon road was also used to trail cattle from the Williams Fork and Dunckley ranches to the railroad at Yampa.

The Dunckley townsite is six miles north of the pass, while Dunckley Park is a high meadow two miles north of the town of Dunckley and southwest of today's town of Oak Creek. A post office was opened in the late 1890s and several stores and schools were built and used in this town. A stagecoach carrying the U.S. mail and supplies for the Dunckley ranches arrived twice a week.

5
BUFFALO PASS

GPS Location: N 40° 28' 28" W 106° 16' 33"
Elevation: 10,320 feet
First road over top: 1895
County: Jackson/Routt
Routt National Forest
On the Continental Divide

Buffalo Pass is the northernmost Continental Divide pass in Colorado and is located on the south end of the Park Range Mountains. The earliest recorded wagon use of this trail was in the mid-1860s. The first stage coach and freight wagon road over the pass was built from today's town of Steamboat Springs to today's town of Walden in North Park in 1895. The road was used to haul grain and other supplies into and out of North Park. From 1890 to 1920, this road was the main route to cross the Continental Divide from Fort Collins and Walden into Steamboat Springs and the Yampa River Valley.

The pass earned its name from the herds of buffalo migrating each year between the Yampa River Valley and North Park. The Ute Indians would set up an ambush in this wooded crossing to easily harvest their winter meat.

Buffalo Pass was no longer maintained or used for crossing the Divide after the Muddy Pass and Rabbit Ears Pass roads were constructed and opened for vehicle traffic.

6
RABBIT EARS PASS

GPS Location: N 40° 23' 05" W 106° 36' 42"
Elevation: 9,426 feet
First road over top: 1876
County: Grand/Jackson
Routt National Forest
On the Continental Divide

In 1969, the USGS Board on Geographic Names officially named this pass "Rabbit Ears." There are twin rocks on a peak two miles north of the pass that look like rabbit ears. The rocks are the remnants of an old volcanic plug.

Lieutenant John Charles Fremont was selected to lead several expeditions of the U.S. Army Corps of Topographical Engineers to find passes in the Colorado Rockies useable for the military and for settlers. Returning from his second journey in 1844, he crossed the Muddy Pass Summit on the Rabbit Ears Range then followed nearby Muddy Creek south to the Colorado River.

In 1873 the topographer Archibald Marvine led the Hayden Surveyors over Muddy Pass, which along with Rabbit Ears Pass, provided the main crossing between North and Middle Parks.

Rabbit Ears Pass was first used by the Ute Indians following the buffalo trail, and the first known white men to use this trail were the fur trappers and traders like William Ashley, Thomas Fitzgerald, "Peg-Leg" Smith, Jim Bridger, Kit Carson, and "Old" Bill Williams. In 1862 prospectors found gold along the Continental Divide.

The first road built over the pass was a U.S. Forest Service Road in 1913 and it was improved in 1919. One half of the costs to build this wagon road came from the U.S. Government. The rest of the money came from private funds donated by settlers needing supplies and from the sheepmen who had been using the Indian trail to move their sheep to pasture. Eventually the Routt County Commissioners reimbursed in full all the contributors that they could find.

The construction of the new paved highway was begun in 1957 and completed in August of 1959. During the construction and paving of Highway 40, traffic was routed over Gore Pass.

The junction of State Highway 14 and U.S. Highway 40 is at the Muddy Pass summit. At that junction Highway 40 crossed the Continental Divide to the Eastern Slope

NORTHWEST COLORADO

The set of rocks to the right is Rabbit Ears Peak.

of the Rockies. At the eastern summit of the pass, Highway 40 crosses back over the Divide and continues west on the Western Slope.

A highway department sign on U. S. Highway 40 at the Continental Divide states that the elevation of Rabbit Ears Pass is 9,426 feet above sea level. It also shows that this is the dividing point of the Pacific and Atlantic watersheds. A little north and west of this sign is a rock pillar holding a bronze plaque. It reads, Rabbit Ears Pass – elevation 9,680 feet. It is located on the early unpaved Rabbit Ears Pass Road built in 1919.

7
MUDDY PASS

GPS Location: N 39° 16' 53" W 106° 34' 47"
Elevation: 8,710 feet
First road over top: 1844
County: Grand/Jackson
Arapaho/Routt National Forest
On the Continental Divide

The trader Rufus B. Sage arrived in Colorado in the fall of 1842. In early December he left North Park over Muddy Pass into Middle Park. He gives us the first written account that Muddy Pass was a large, wide, and flat mountain crossing.

NORTHWEST COLORADO

Muddy Pass is named for the nearby Muddy Creek flowing south, a tributary of the Colorado River. The creek begins on the west side of the Continental Divide above today's Dumont Lake and joins the Colorado at today's town of Kremmling. Muddy Pass is the lowest crossing over the Continental Divide in Colorado.

Captain John Fremont led a division of the U.S. Army's "Corps of Topographical Engineers" from St. Louis into the Colorado Rockies in mid-June of 1842. Their goal was to map the Oregon Trail as far as South Pass in Wyoming. Fremont and his men were back in St. Louis by mid-October of 1842.

In May of 1843, Fremont's second expedition, with Kit Carson as guide, left Missouri for today's Colorado. They arrived at the spot of the future Denver in early July. They continued west across Nevada's Great Basin and reached California on February 20, 1844. After completing their military business, they returned to Colorado. They entered Colorado's North Park where they crossed the Continental Divide, using Muddy Pass to enter Middle Park. Muddy Pass is shown on a Middle Park map printed in 1859.

In 1873, the Hayden Surveyors topographer Archibald Marvine's party charted Muddy Pass. He was joined in Middle Park by Dr. Hayden and Photographer William H. Jackson. He led his men to the Flattops following Ute Indian trails. There they mapped the mountains, naming Big and Little Marvine Peaks, west of Trappers Lake, and Marvine Lake and Creek.

Today's State Highway 14 heads south from Walden and ends at the summit of Muddy Pass. Today's U.S. Highway 40, coming north from Kremmling, crosses the Muddy Pass summit. U.S. 40 continues west to cross Rabbit Ears Pass and down to the town of Steamboat Springs.

8
GORE PASS

GPS Location: N 40° 04' 33" W 106° 33' 39"
Elevation: 9,524 feet
First road over top: 1867
County: Grand
Arapaho/Routt National Forest

Who is this man with his name on many geographic locations in Colorado? We have the Gore Mountain Range that extends from just south of Rabbit Ears Pass heading south to the Silverthorne/ Vail Pass area and Ten Mile Canyon, Gore Mountain, Gore Creek, Gore Pass, and Gore Canyon on the upper Colorado River.

He is Sir Saint George Gore, a Baronet from Sligo, Ireland. The word "Saint" in his name is one of history's unexplainable mysteries. He was born in 1811 in County Donegal. He had been educated at Winchester and at Oriel College in Oxford, England. His rank of Baronet in Irish Royalty was below that of a Baron, but above the rank of a Knight. He arrived in St. Louis in 1853 and at Fort Laramie, Wyoming, in the spring of 1854. It was probably there that he hired Jim Bridger and Joseph Chatillon to be his hunting guides. Gore started his hunting in Wyoming and stayed the winter of 1854-55. In the spring of 1855 they followed the North Platte River out of Wyoming into Colorado to its headwaters near today's town of Walden.

Written history states that Gore and Bridger built the first wagon road over today's Gore Mountain Range. The "Mountain Men's Middle Park Map" of 1859 shows this crossing of the Gore Range as an un-named pass. H. M. Vaile claims to have named the pass "Gore" in 1863.

A rusted tin can was found on a mountain top in the Gore Range. It had been used by mountain climbers to record their arrival on the range, and on the note in the can was the signature of Major John Wesley Powell. His climb of the Gore Range was described on the front page of the *Chicago Tribune's* edition of October 4, 1868.

The number of people and animals in Gore's hunting party vary among historians. It is written that Gore rode in a fancy wagon that also carried his large striped tent as cover for his bed, portable bathtub, and other furniture. He had one hundred plus men, about one hundred horses, many wagons with five yokes of oxen each, forty to fifty hounds, a large arsenal of weapons and ammunition, and carts full of champagne.

The wide range of animals killed by Gore included buffalo, elk, deer, and bear plus small game such as grouse, rabbits, ducks, and geese. What did they do with all of the meat? His crew would require meat for three meals a day. They could have traded the hides and some of the meat with their Ute neighbors.

It is also recorded that in the evenings he would meet with his guides for planning. He liked to read Shakespeare to Bridger and share the champagne cooled in the mountain streams.

Many years ago a brass plaque was erected on top of the pass. It reads:

Gore Pass
Altitude 9,000'

Here in 1855 crossed Sir St. George Gore, an Irish Baronet bent on slaughter of game, and guided by Jim Bridger. For three years he scoured Colorado, Montana, and Wyoming accompanied usually by forty men, many carts, wagons, hounds and unexampled camp luxuries. More than 2,000 buffalo, 1,600 elk and deer, 100 bear were massacred for sport. A trail by 1866, a wagon road by 1874, this modern highway opened in 1956.

CONTINENTAL DIVIDE—NORTHERN COLORADO

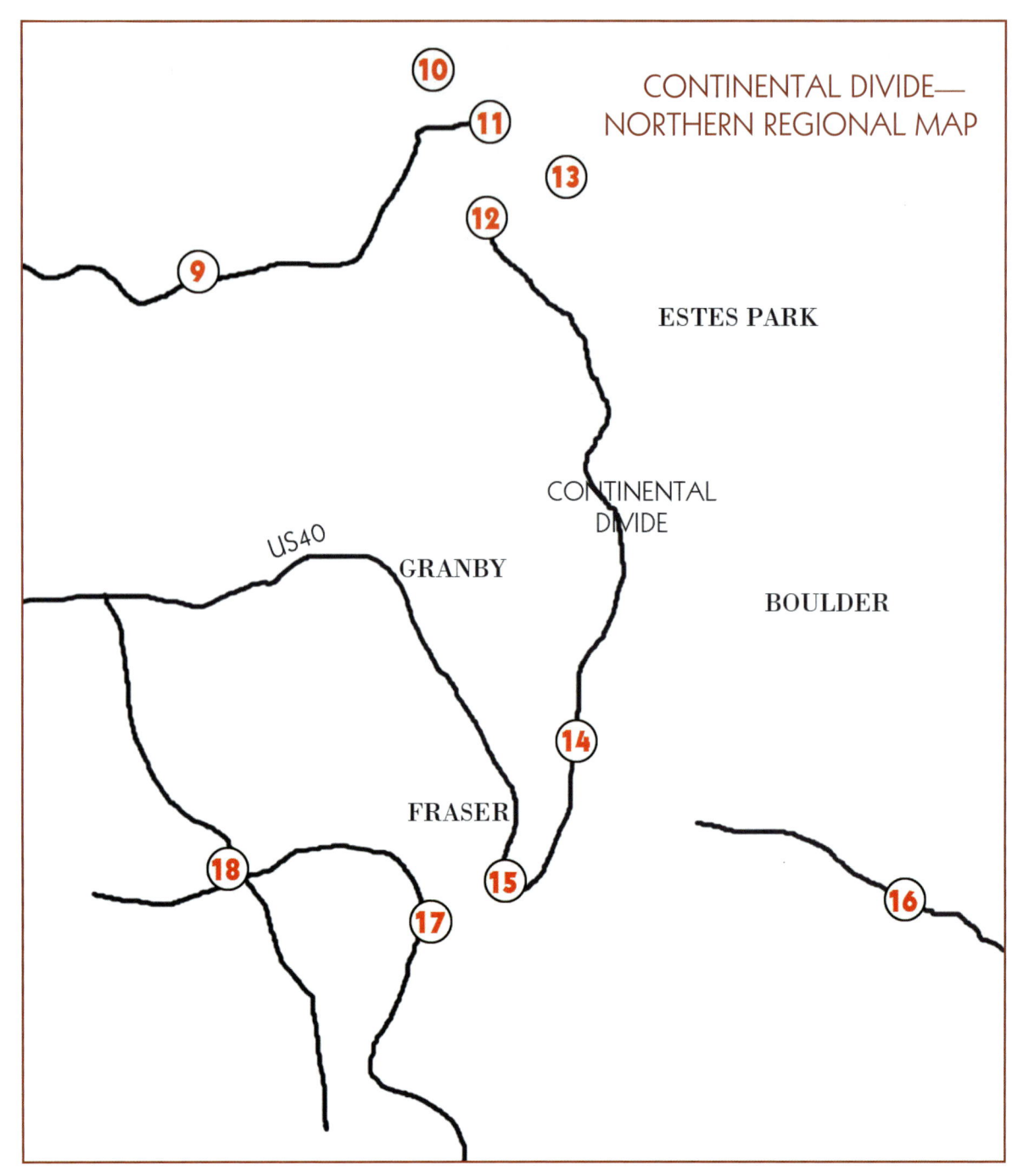

9	Willow Creek Pass	15	Berthoud Pass
10	Cameron Pass	16	Golden Gate Pass
11	La Poudre Pass	17	Jones Pass
12	Milner Pass	18	Ute Pass (Off Hwy. 9, on Hwy. 132)
13	Fall River Pass		
14	Rollins Pass		

CONTINENTAL DIVIDE—NORTHERN COLORADO

9
WILLOW CREEK PASS

GPS Location: N 40° 21' 02" W 106° 05' 32"
Elevation: 9,621 feet
Road over top: 1902
County: Grand/Jackson
Arapaho/Rout National Forest
On the divide

In the summer of 1873, the Hayden Survey team, led by topographer Archibald Marvine, charted three Ute Indian trails crossing the Continental Divide between North Park and Middle Park. They named the passes Muddy, Troublesome, and Willow Creek. From Willow Creek Marvine led his men north on hunting trails to today's Flat Tops. They named Big and Little Marvine Peaks, Marvine Lakes, and Marvine Creek. Some of the other peaks that they named are Trappers, Rat, Shingle, Turret, and Timber.

This pass was named after Willow Creek for the creek's headwaters near its summit. The road crosses the Rabbit Ears Range on the Continental Divide. It is reported that in the summer of 1882 prospectors were working placer claims in Willow Creek. The dictionary defines "placer" as "an alluvial marine or glacial deposit into the earth which contains particles of valuable minerals, especially of gold." Early placer mining in rivers and streams was called "panning." The use of dredges in the rivers enabled prospectors to bring up larger quantities of gold bearing ore. The placer mining in Willow Creek was not successful. The only profitable placer mining in Colorado was on the Blue River near Breckenridge and at Fairplay in South Park.

The buffalo and Ute Indian trail was changed into a wagon road for wheeled vehicles in 1902. A stagecoach line, owned by H. Loucks of Walden, ran regularly over Willow Creek Pass to connect Walden with the town of Granby. Dave and Mrs. A. L. Gresham operated a roadhouse on the pass to provide meals and lodging for travelers.

The major issue for the United States in the 1920s was prohibition. A law was created and passed forbidding the manufacture, transportation, and sale of alcoholic liquors. Two exceptions were allowed, liquids made for medical and sacramental usage.

In Colorado a state amendment installing prohibition was adopted as law on January 1, 1916. The manufacture of home brew, white lightning, and corn whiskey went underground. Little distilleries were easily concealed in a lodgepole pine forest in the mining areas of the Continental Divide. The "bootlegging" manufacturing of alcohol was heaviest in the Fraser River Valley and in the upper basins of Willow Creek.

CONTINENTAL DIVIDE—NORTHERN COLORADO

10
CAMERON PASS

GPS Location: N 40° 31'15" W 105° 53' 33"
Elevation: 10,276 feet
First road over top: 1882
County: Jackson/Larimer
Roosevelt/Routt National Forest

General Robert A. Cameron came to Colorado in 1870 to become the Vice President and Superintendent of Nathan Meeker's Union Colony at Greeley. Cameron was in charge of greeting and locating people in this new agriculture colony. The treasurer of Union Colony was Horace Greeley, owner and publisher of the New York Tribune newspaper. In 1872 Cameron started another agriculture colony at Fort Collins and later started the Fountain Colony at Colorado Springs.

During his time at the Union Colony he explored the headwaters of the Poudre River. Fur traders had traveled up the Poudre from Fort Collins using the trail that went to Cameron Pass on the Continental Divide. When the Union Pacific Railroad surveyors crossed this area they named the pass for Cameron.

Robert Cameron discovered this trail over the Medicine Bow Mountain Range in the early 1870s. A toll road was built on the trail route and opened for business in 1882. A stage coach line carried passengers and the U.S. Mail from Fort Collins over Cameron Pass to Teller City and beyond. Prospectors used this route to reach the mining areas in North and Middle Parks. Improvements were made to upgrade this road in 1913, and it was made an automobile road in 1926, today's State Highway 14.

11
LA POUDRE PASS

GPS Location: N 40° 28' 36" W 105° 49' 24"
Elevation: 10,192 feet
First road over top: Early 1870s
County: Grand/Larimer
Roosevelt National Forest/Rocky Mountain National Park
On the Divide
No road over top today

In 1932 this pass was named by the USGS Board on Geographic Names for the nearby headwaters of the La Poudre River. The river was named by French trappers working for the American Fur Company. In order to lighten the loads of their wagon teams, they buried a stash of gun powder kegs close to the river and called it "Cache La Poudre." Poudre is the French word for powder.

CONTINENTAL DIVIDE—NORTHERN COLORADO

This remarkable pass has the headwaters of the La Poudre River on the north side of the Continental Divide and the headwaters of the Colorado River on the south side.

During the Lulu City mining boom from 1879 to 1881 in the North Fork Valley of the Colorado River, Fort Collins stage coaches would cross over this pass on the La Poudre Wagon Road. In 1881 a regular mail route crossed La Poudre Pass. La Poudre Pass is identified on an 1883 mountain map, but not on today's U.S.G.S. topo maps.

The Grand River Ditch collects water from the Never Summer Mountain Range and carries it across the Continental Divide on La Poudre Pass where the water flows into Long Draw Reservoir. This fourteen mile long ditch starts in Bakers Gulch, goes north past Lulu City at a slant to keep the channel reasonably clean and then into Long Draw Reservoir. Today, in the late summer water is released into the La Poudre River for today's Fort Collins farmers to use for the last irrigation of their sugar beets.

12
MILNER PASS

GPS Location: N 40° 25' 11" W 105° 48' 41"
Elevation: 10,758 feet
First road over Top: 1920
County: Grand/Larimer
In Rocky Mountain National Park
On the Divide

The first road west across today's Rocky Mountain National Park from the town of Estes Park was the Fall River Road. The Milner Pass Road headed west across the park to cross the Continental Divide on Milner Pass to reach Grand Lake. The Arapaho Indians called this divide pass "Deer Pass." The construction of the Milner Pass road started in September of 1913 and it was finished and opened by the summer of 1920. The road's condition was upgraded in 1932.

The pass is named for T. J. Milner, who was well known and respected by railroad men in Colorado. He was the civil engineer for the City of Leadville in 1880. He was chosen to help with the organizing of the proposed Denver and Salt Lake Western Railroad Company and he was the surveyor for this new route. Willis Lee of the U.S. Geological Survey honored Milner by naming this pass for him.

Rocky Mountain National Park leaders decided to build a new automobile road across the Park. The "Trail Ridge Road" construction started at the town of Estes Park heading north to its highest elevation of 12,183 feet near Fall River Pass. The road builders then headed south to cross the Continental Divide over Milner Pass and continued south to the town of Grand Lake. This road was dedicated and opened in the fall of 1932.

CONTINENTAL DIVIDE—NORTHERN COLORADO

13
FALL RIVER PASS

GPS Location: N 40° 26' 26" W 105° 45' 17"
Elevation: 11,796 feet
First road over top: 1920
County: Larimer
In Rocky Mountain National Park

The Indians crossed Fall River Pass hunting buffalo for winter meat and hides for robes and tent coverings. The Arapaho Indians were still crossing this "Dog Trail" in 1915. They used a drag-behind travois harnessed to a dog to move their belongings and supplies. Mountain trappers and fur traders were the next pass users headed west and east.

Construction began in 1919 to build the Fall River Road from the town of Estes Park on the east side of Rocky Mountain National Park to Grand Lake on the western side. Road construction was started from both ends of the road at the same time. The road was opened for traffic on September 14, 1920. A cloudburst destroyed five miles of the Fall Creek Road on July 23, 1925. When the Trail Ridge Road was opened in 1932, the Fall River Road was opened for one-way uphill traffic. Fall River Pass is not on the Continental Divide. Milner Pass is about four miles southwest of Fall River Pass and is on the Continental Divide.

Chasm Falls can be seen just off the Fall River Pass road which today is a one way road from its beginning to the pass summit.

When Rocky Mountain National Park was created, Governor William H. Adams approved building a new highway for the park. His "Trail Ridge Road" was to replace the steep switchbacks of the old Fall Creek Road. His new park road was opened in the fall of 1932. The highest elevation on Trail Ridge Road is 12,183 feet, making it the highest federal highway in the United States.

14
ROLLINS PASS

GPS Location: N 39° 56' 03"   W 105° 40' 58"
Elevation: 11,660
First road over the top: 1873
County: Boulder/Grand
Arapaho/Roosevelt National Forest
On the Divide

Like most Colorado passes the first people to use this pass were Indians. It was the Utes hunting buffalo, and the Arapaho gathering lodgepole pines for their lodges. The first white men to use this pass and trail were the men in Captain John Fremont's expedition in the summer of 1844.

One summer day in 1865, John Q. A. Rollins started from his mining town called Rollinsville to show friends "The Rollinsville and Middle Park Toll Road." He had just bought the charter to build the road. They rode mules up South Boulder Creek and across the shoulder of James Peak to the top of the Continental Divide.

Rollins started building his wagon road west from Rollinsville in 1866. His forty mile road construction went slow because long winters shortened the window for road work. He built his road over the divide in June of 1873 to connect with today's towns of Fraser, Gramby, and Hot Sulphur Springs. A U.S. mail contract was awarded in 1875 to deliver mail from Rollinsville to Hot Sulphur Springs over Rollins Pass. One

The South Boulder Creek Valley and the townsite of Tolland can be seen in this panorama taken from the east side of the Rollins Pass road.

CONTINENTAL DIVIDE—NORTHERN COLORADO

other fact worth mentioning is that Rollins did not allow saloons, gambling halls, or sporting houses to be built or operate in his town. Rollins continued to invest in mining, real estate, hotels, the Butterfield Stage Company, the South Park Salt Works, and the Berthoud Pass Company.

David H. Moffat, Jr. moved into Omaha, Nebraska in the 1850s, then into Denver in 1860. He worked in banking and railroading in several areas of Colorado. Then Governor John Evans hired Moffat to incorporate the Denver, South Park and Pacific Railroad in 1873. On July 18, 1902, at the age of sixty-three, Moffat incorporated his own railroad, The Denver, Northwestern and Pacific Railway.

He chose to use John Rollins' wagon road, hiring the locating engineer H. A. Sumner to set the grades for his rails. His "High Line" rails were laid up South Boulder Creek and through the towns of Tolland and Rollinsville to Rollins Pass on the top of the Continental Divide. The rails reached the pass in June of 1904. Moffat built a railroad station on the pass which was called Corona, Spanish for "crest."

Starting down the west side of the Divide the construction crews reached the town of Arrow in September of 1904 and the town of Fraser in the fall of 1904. The rails were laid to Granby in the summer of 1905, and to Kremmling in 1906. In the summer of 1908, the rails were in place through State Bridge, Toponos, Yampa, Oak Creek, and into Steamboat Springs. Long winters and poor financing slowed down the rail laying. On November 20, 1913, the final rails were operational from Steamboat to Craig.

The Rollins Pass road skirts around Yankee Doodle Lake.

CONTINENTAL DIVIDE—NORTHERN COLORADO

From the summit looking north, the Berthoud Pass road descends into the Fraser River Valley. The Front Range can be seen in the background.

15
BERTHOUD PASS

GPS Location: N 39° 47' 54" W 105° 46' 40"
Elevation: 11,315 feet
First Road over top: November, 1874
County: Clear Creek/ Grand
Arapahao National Forest

In March of 1860, a graduate of New York's Union College arrived in Golden, Colorado, with his wife and an engineering degree. Captain Edward Berthoud's resume included working as a surveyor on the railroad built across the Isthmus of Panama. His first job in Colorado was to survey William A. H. Loveland's wagon road that headed west along Clear Creek.

The Central Overland Stage Company wanted the government's contract to carry U.S. mail from Denver to California. They hired the topographical wizard Jim Bridger to find a pass over the Continental Divide on which they would build a wagon road and win the contract. Bridger heard about Berthoud, contacted him, and they joined forces. They headed up West Clear Creek to look at Jones and Vasquez Passes on the Continental Divide for possible road crossings. They spotted a third gap which they reached on May 12, 1861. It was an excellent low crossing for a road, with a stream flowing west just over the summit. The stream is the headwaters of today's Fraser River. When they reported this pass as the best choice for a stagecoach crossing, they were hired to survey a wagon road route from Denver to Salt Lake City. Berthoud named the new pass "Central Overland." His employers named it Berthoud's Pass.

In June of 1874, Ex-Governor John Evans took William N. Byers, the owner and editor of Denver's newspaper named the *Rocky Mountain News*, to the top of Berthoud Pass. Evans wanted Byers to join him in building a good modern road over the Continental Divide. The construction of that wagon road was started in July and opened in November of 1874. A Concord stagecoach made the first trip on the new road. This pass road was the main route between Eastern Colorado and Middle Park during the late 1870s and the early 1880s.

The first telephone service crossed Berthoud Pass in 1903. In 1924 the road was improved to become part of the "Victory Highway" honoring American success in World War I. It was later designated part of U.S. Highway 40 and was the first paved crossing of the Continental Divide.

16
GOLDEN GATE ROAD AND PASS

GPS Location:
Elevation: 7,754 feet
First road over top: 1859
County: Gilpin
Public access through private land

The Ute Indians used a trail through this area to travel to the plains. The Arapaho Indians used their "Arapaho Trail" to get lodge poles for their tents and wild game for food.

Three prospectors set their camp on the site of today's town of Golden in the fall of 1858. Their names were Tom Golden, George A. Jackson, and James Saunders. On January 7, 1859, Jackson discovered gold high in a gulch near North Clear Creek close to today's Idaho Springs. On May 6, 1859, John H. Gregory discovered gold on the North Fork of Clear Creek near today's town of Black Hawk. Some of the "Georgian" Forty-Niners became Colorado's Fifty-Niners and the gold rush was on. John Gregory built the first wagon road into his mining area and named it the Golden Gate Road. One of his first companions into the Central City area was a prospector named H. A. W. Tabor.

Our three prospectors named the new town being built at their campsite "Golden." The mining camp of Golden Gate City at the entrance to Golden Gate Canyon was the toll gate for the road. Two tall free-standing rocks on the north side of the canyon, looking a little like a gate, were destroyed when someone trying to improve the road accidentally knocked them down. The town of Golden was founded in June of 1859 and Golden Gate City in December of 1859.

Leaving Golden the Golden Gate Road heads west through Golden Gate Canyon and up to the top of Guy Hill. It then crossed Golden Gate Pass and headed down to Guy Gulch. John Guy was the first settler to homestead along this road. The next mountain crossed by the Golden Gate Road is named "Michigan Hill." The road continues across a valley to use the Dory Hill shortcut. It turns south for 8½ miles to enter Black Hawk and Central City.

The Golden Gate Road, about thirty-eight miles long, was the first direct route from Denver to Black Hawk and Central City.

17
JONES PASS

GPS Location: N 39° 46' 25"   W 105° 53' 21"
Elevation: 12,451 feet
First road over top: 1873
County: Clear Creek/Grand
Arapaho National Forest
On the Divide

This pass is named for John S. Jones, an early mine owner, freighter, and road builder in the upper Clear Creek Mining District. He built a road up West Clear Creek to make it possible to travel from his home and mill in Empire over the Continental Divide to

Jones Pass road runs west from the Berthoud Pass road, past the Henderson Mine, and continues past Vasquez Peak until it reaches the summit. A short distance past the summit, the Jones Pass road is closed and gated.

CONTINENTAL DIVIDE—NORTHERN COLORADO

his ranch near Hot Sulphur Springs on the Colorado River. The road started at the west end of Berthoud Falls at the base of the Berthoud Pass road on today's U.S. Highway 40. When the Hayden Survey party visited this pass in 1873, they reported a good wagon road crossed the pass into Middle Park and ended at the start of the Williams Fork River.

In 1938 work was started on a two-mile tunnel under Jones Pass that would divert water from the Williams Fork River on the west side of the Continental Divide into Clear Creek on the east side of the divide. The Denver Parks Department opened a road over the pass in 1938 to provide access to both ends of the tunnel from the east. In 1940 water was running through the tunnel. In 1965 the tunnel was named the August P. Gumlick Tunnel for a member of the Denver Water Board.

Today's Jones Pass Road from the east goes up a mining valley and passes the huge Climax-Henderson Molybdenum Mine opened in 1976. The mine is on the east side of the divide and the mill is located on the west side of the Continental Divide. The mine and the mill are connected by the world's longest conveyor belt, a fifteen-mile long elevated belt that passes under the divide from the mine to the mill. The Henderson Mine is near the Urad Mine, which produced molybdenum from 1914 to the 1960s. The Henderson Mine is North America's largest producer of primary molybdenum, which is used for the strengthening of steel.

18
UTE PASS
(OFF HWY. 9, ON HWY. 132)

GPS Location: N 39° 49' 27" W 106° 06' 19"
Elevation: 9,568 feet
First road over top: early 1900s
County: Grand/Summit
Arapaho National Forest

This pass was named Ute because it is part of the east/west Old Ute Indian Trail located in Northern Colorado. This low pass road heads northwest out of Silverthorne in the Blue River Valley on today's Highway 9. The road turns north along Pass Creek to cross the Williams Fork Mountain Range three miles north of Ute Peak and drops into the Williams Fork River Valley. Continuing north, the road goes up to today's Williams Fork Reservoir and the town of Parshall on U.S. Highway 40.

In a journal kept by stagecoach travelers in 1862, they wrote about the boggy marsh on the east side of the pass and about the abundant wildlife that provided fresh meat for their meals. It is probable that the first road over the pass was not built until the early 1900s.

GUNNISON COUNTRY

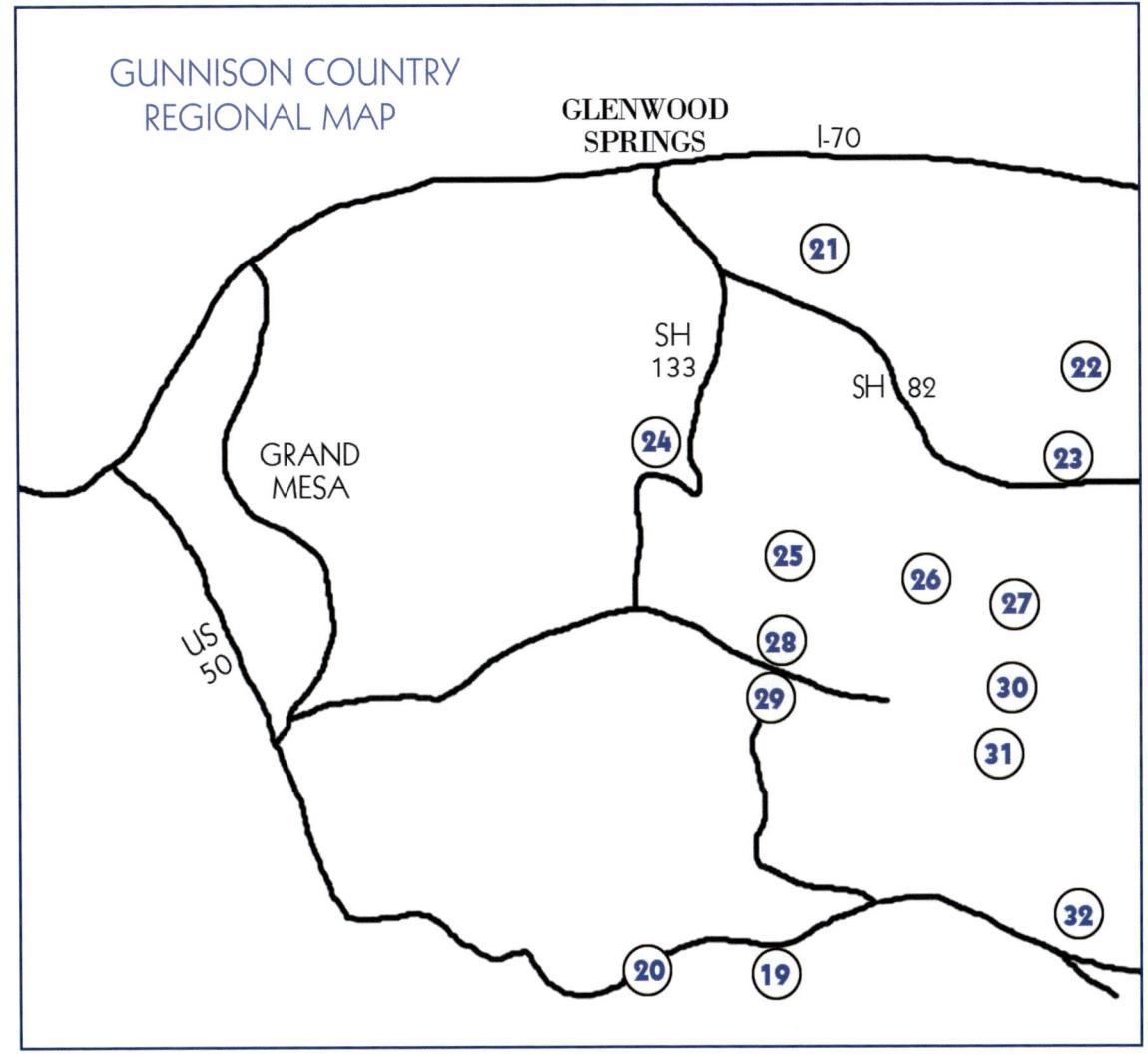

19	Blue Mesa Summit	27	Taylor Pass
20	Cerro Summit	28	Kebler Pass
21	Cottonwood Pass (South of Gypsum)	29	Ohio Pass
		30	Tincup Pass
22	Hagerman Pass	Towns of Virginia City and Tincup	
23	Independence Pass	31	Cumberland Pass
24	McClure Pass	32	Waunita Pass
25	Schofield Pass	Town of Pitkin	
26	Pearl Pass		

59

19
BLUE MESA SUMMIT

GPS Location: N 38° 23' 58" W106° 27' 06"
Elevation: 8,704 feet
First road over top: August, 1853
County: Gunnison
Public access through private land

A Ute Indian trail headed west followed the Gunnison River past today's Curecanti Needle. It is a cone-shaped rock with an elevation of about 7,900 feet, named for the Ute Indian Chief Curicata. When the trail reached today's Cimarron River Canyon, it went upstream to today's town of Cimarron to cross Cerro Summit.

Written history tells us that the first non-Indian to cross Blue Mesa Summit was Antoine Robidoux. He was a French trader who arrived from Santa Fe to build a trading post on the Gunnison River near its confluence with the Uncompahgre River. It is possible that he was the one who named the hill going up out of the Black Canyon the "Son-of-a-Bitch" Trail.

In the mid-1840s, Lt. John Charles Fremont followed the Indian trail over Blue Mesa Summit and Cerro Summit while headed for California.

In 1853, Captain John Gunnison's survey party entered the Black Canyon of today's Gunnison River near Sapinero. He led his men and wagons for about ten miles, then chose to use the "S.O.B. Hill" to climb out of the canyon. Continuing west they reached the Green River in Utah in September, 1853. They crossed the Wasatch Mountains into the Sevier River Valley arriving on October 26. Unfortunately they chose to camp where a wagon train party had recently killed a Paiute Indian chief. To get even the Indians attacked at dawn, killing Gunnison and seven of his men.

In the mid-1870s, Dr. Hayden's surveyors measured and mapped the entire Gunnison River Valley.

In 1875, Otto Mears chartered a toll road to be built west from the Lake Fork of the Gunnison River to the town of Cimarron. In 1877, he continued the road to the new Ute Indian Agency at today's town of Colona. He continued his toll road south along the Uncompahgre River to its terminus at Ouray. In 1881, settlers crossed Blue Mesa Summit on their way to homestead in the Uncompahgre River Valley. The Ute Indians had been moved out and relocated because of the Meeker Massacre on the White River.

Today's topographic and Forest Service maps do not show the Blue Mesa Summit where Gunnison crossed and Otto Mears built his toll road. That summit is under the water of Blue Mesa Reservoir. U.S. 50 today follows Big Blue Creek to the top of Blue Mesa and Little Cimarron Creek to the town of Cimarron.

20
CERRO SUMMIT

GPS Location: N 38° 26' 43" W 107° 38' 28"
Elevation: 7,950 feet
First road over top: 1875
County: Montrose
Public use through private land

The Spanish word for a mountain ridge is "Cerro." This pass is a low pass over a mesa. Written history does not tell us who named it "Cerro Summit."

The French fur trapper Antoine Robidoux followed the Ute Indian highway across Cerro in the late 1820s. He planned to build a trading post near the confluence of today's Gunnison and Uncompahgre Rivers. When completed he named it "Fort Robidoux." He supplied food, clothing, and other supplies to the settlers passing through in wagon trains, the mountain men, and trappers.

In 1853, Captain John Gunnison's Army Topographers crossed Cerro on their search for an intercontinental railway route through Colorado's Rocky Mountains.

In 1875, the Ute Indians were to be moved from the Los Piños Agency west of Cochetopa Pass to a new agency on the Uncompahgre River near today's town of Colona. Otto Mears bought the charter to build a wagon road to make this move possible. During the summers of 1875 and 1876, he built his wagon road from the town of Barnum on the Lake Fork of the Gunnison River to the Gunnison River. He built west along the Gunnison, crossing Blue Mesa and Cerro Summit to the Uncompahgre River and the new Indian agency. He completed his toll road by building it south into the town of Ouray.

Palmer's Denver and Rio Grande goal, after arriving in Gunnison, was to build his railroad to the junction of the Gunnison River with the Grand River. If he could have built rails through the Black Canyon, it would have been a shorter route to today's town of Grand Junction but the canyon became impassable and it was impossible to continue to build rails. They did reach the canyon of the Cimarron River which gave them a way to build out of the Black Canyon. At the top they built a railroad town and named it Cimarron. Then they built west over Cerro Summit to today's town of Montrose, and north into Grand Junction.

GUNNISON COUNTRY

21
COTTONWOOD PASS
(SOUTH OF GYPSUM)

GPS Location: N 39° 31' 50" W 107° 03' 29"
Elevation: 8,280 feet
First road over Top: 1883
County: Eagle
Public access through private land

Today's Cottonwood Pass Road starts on U.S. Highway 24 in Gypsum. The road is called "Cottonwood Pass Road" up to the pass summit. After crossing the pass, the road follows and is named "Cattle Creek." The road was built using an early Indian trail to cross the divide. Most of the road today is a graveled two-lane road with about 35 per cent of the road being one-lane switchbacks or shelf road.

When U.S. 24 was being built through Glenwood Canyon in 1937, the Cottonwood Pass Road was the detour route for the Denver to Grand Junction traffic. When I-70 was in the works, the Colorado Department of Transportation again looked at Cottonwood as a detour road. They decided however that it would cost too much to build a detour road capable of handling semi-truck traffic.

22
HAGERMAN PASS
(STORY OF THE TUNNELS)

GPS Location: N 39° 16' 06.4" W 106° 25' 00"
Elevation: 11,925 feet
First road over the top: 1887
County: Lake/Pitkin
White River/San Isabel National Forest
On the Divide
Pass requires high clearance four wheel drive vehicle.

The tunnel story begins in the summer of 1887 when the Colorado Midland Railroad's construction crews laid twenty-five miles of rails from Leadville to the Continental Divide. Hagerman's railway locating engineer had found and surveyed the lowest crossing over the Divide at the elevation of 11,925 feet. Because of heavy snows and high winds the railroad could not operate during Colorado winters. Plans were drawn for a tunnel to be built at the elevation of 11,528 feet. The construction was started for the 2,060 foot tunnel in the summer of 1885 and it was completed on August 30, 1887. The first train came through the tunnel that same day. The tunnel was named Hagerman.

Today, the west portal of the Hagerman Tunnel has collapsed and is flooded. The railroad bed leading from the tunnel is still blackened by soot from the engines.

Later the company built snow sheds on each end of the tunnel to keep the tracks open. Winter snows again closed the rails on both sides of Hagerman Pass.

In May of 1890, James J. Hagerman's health forced him to stop serving as President of the Colorado Midland and sell his ownership of the railroad.

The Midland's directors decided to build a tunnel at a lower elevation. The Busk Tunnel Railway Company was incorporated on June 14, 1890 to build this tunnel. It was to be built by a private contractor and leased to the Midland upon completion. The contract for construction was given to Michael H. Keefe of Helena, Montana. Construction was started on the new Busk-Ivanhoe Tunnel on July 26, 1890. Two construction camps were built for material storage and workers housing. The camp at the east portal was called Busk. J. R. Busk was a major stockholder of the Colorado Midland Railroad. The main work camp at the west portal was named Ivanhoe. The tunnel was to be bored at the elevation of 10,947 feet at the west portal and 10,810 feet at the east portal. The tunnel was to be 9,395 feet long, fifteen feet in width, and twenty-one feet in height. The elevation drop between the portals gave the tunnel good water drainage. The tunnel was completed on October 18, 1893.

In one of William Jackson's photographs of the tunnel's east portal construction a trail is visible heading up to the summit of the Continental Divide. It was the burro trail used to carry supplies over the top to the west portal. The crossing was called "Wigglesworth," named for the Midland's locating engineer Thomas P. Wigglesworth.

GUNNISON COUNTRY

While descending from the west portal of the Hagerman Tunnel, this view of Ivanhoe Lake can be seen.

It is reported that Michael Keefe's construction company expanded this burro trail into a wagon road in order to move men and materials over the Divide. It is probable that they used the Hagerman Tunnel to move supplies over to the west portal. Large derricks were erected to lift the rails, ties and boring machinery for drilling the tunnel.

The railroad started using the Busk-Ivanhoe Tunnel on December 13, 1893 and the Hagerman Tunnel was closed in January of 1894. On April 21, 1917, A. E. Carlton bought the Midland Railway. In 1921, the rails were removed and the tunnel was used for automobiles. The tunnel was closed in 1930.

23
INDEPENDENCE PASS

GPS Location: N 39° 06' 32" W 106° 33' 50"
Elevation: 12,095 feet
First road over top: 1881
County: Lake/Pitkin
San Isabel/White River National Forest
On the Continental Divide

The first white men to use this wide open crossing above timberline were Captain Zebulon Pike's Party in 1806. Dr. Hayden's surveyors mapped and measured here in the summer of 1874.

In 1865, Ira King and other Ohio prospectors traveled west from the Arkansas River Valley to start a mining district at the Upper Lake Inlet. They called it the "Red Mountain Mining District" and called their tent city "Dayton." The lake was one of two lakes, today's "Twin Lakes." They discovered a complex galena ore rich in silver. In 1866 Dayton was a town of over 400 people with the first Lake County Court House set up in a Masonic Hall. The mining boom ended by 1868 and most residents moved to Granite.

Following the Leadville Silver Boom in 1877 and '78, miners went south and west. In 1879, Dayton was reborn as Twin Lakes. Miners coming through climbed up to and over the pass called "Hunter." They built a tent city four miles down on the west side of the pass. On July 4, 1879, they struck gold ore. They named their town and the pass Independence. Stores and housing were built and a stamp mill was constructed for crushing ore to be carried out by a "Jack Train."

In 1880, B. Clark Wheeler started building the first road over the pass from Aspen. A survey was made for the toll road to be built from Twin Lakes to Aspen. Wheeler built his twenty mile road to the top of the pass by the end of 1881. At the same time, work was started on the Twin Lakes side by Dr. J. E. "Doc" Rice, who built the east side of the road up the North Branch of Lake Creek to the top of the pass. The road over the pass was officially opened on November 6, 1881. The length of the road from Twin Lakes to Aspen was forty-three miles. All through that winter the road was kept open by use of sleighs and a "shovel army." Summertime came to the top of Independence Pass revealing virtual wetlands. It became necessary to build a wooden plank

The Independence Pass road climbs the west side of the Continental Divide to the pass summit.

GUNNISON COUNTRY

The townsite of Independence today is being restored and is open for exploration during the summer months.

road ten to twelve feet wide using rocks and "green" timber. The road was capable of only one-way traffic and when two freight wagons would meet, one of them would have to leave the road and go into the mud. The decision as to which vehicle got the right-of-way was settled by a "fist-fight" between the two drivers. Pardon the pun—but losing the fight hurt in more ways than one! The next summer, mail and stage service was started between Aspen and Leadville, and daily stages ran between Buena Vista through Granite and Twin Lakes into Aspen.

In 1912 the Forest Service started building a new road over the pass using the 1881 right-of-way. In 1915, Colorado's Governor E. M. Ammons and the state highway engineer took a ride over the pass road. They agreed that it was time for a hard-surfaced road. The state, county, and federal governments provided the financing, and the road was completed in 1927 at the cost of $475,000. This pass road is today's Highway 82, running from Ball Town on Highway 24 to Aspen Town.

24
McCLURE PASS

GPS Location: N 39° 07' 44" W 107° 17' 02"
Elevation: 8,763 feet
First road over top: 1947
County: Gunnison/Pitkin
Gunnison/White River National Forest

During 1886, a wagon road was built north from the townsite of Schofield following Rock Creek, today's Crystal River, through Crystal City and Marble to the area at the foot of today's McClure Pass. Thomas "Mack" McClure, an Irish farmer, built a large house where he fed and lodged travelers. He called it the McClure House, and the area around him was called McClure Flats. McClure's farm was bordered by the Crystal River on the east side and the mountains on the west side. McClure developed and introduced a new variety of potato called the Red McClure. It was a potato that could be grown at high altitudes and in the Crystal River Valley's red alluvial soil.

A trail had been used by the Ute Indians to cross the Rock Creek/Muddy Creek Divide. The December 7, 1917, edition of the *Paonian* newspaper reported that the survey for the proposed McClure Pass Road had been completed. Ranchers and citizens on both sides of the pass began raising funds to build the road. The contractors were hired, Axelson and Lemay for the eight miles of road on the west side of the pass, and Adair Rippy's Construction Company for the two miles on the east side. The road on the east side of the pass required many sharp switchbacks which can still be seen today. On July 13, 1947, the wagon road over the top was completed. Today Highway 133 crosses McClure Pass.

Sections of the first pass road can be seen in the middle of this picture. Highway 133 and the Crystal River are in the lower right corner.

From the west side of McClure Pass, we see Chair Mountain on the left and the Ragged Mountain range.

GUNNISON COUNTRY

25
SCHOFIELD PASS

GPS Location: N 39° 00' 54" W 107° 02' 48"
Elevation: 10,707 feet
First road over top: 1883
County: Gunnison
Gunnison/White River National Forest
Pass requires high clearance four wheel drive vehicle

Dr. F. V. Hayden led his surveyors to map and measure today's western Gunnison County in the mid-1870s. They headed north from today's town of Crested Butte on the trail to the mining town of Gothic. The trail continued north around Emerald Lake and crossed a divide using a pass into a mountain park. A mining townsite was started next to the headwaters of Rock Creek on the north end of the park. Judge B. F. Schofield directed the platting of this new town in the summer of 1879, and the town, pass, and park were named Schofield.

In August of 1880, ex-Colorado Governor J. L. Routt took ex-President Ulysses Grant by wagon from Gunnison to see the Gothic area. They rode mules into Schofield.

From Crested Butte through Gothic and past Perry Park, a road passes Emerald Lake to reach the summit of Schofield Pass.

The townsite of Schofield was at the north end of Schofield Park. The Crystal River canyon starts here. Please heed the signs!

From the town, the Rock Creek canyon went downstream on a twenty-seven degree pitch to today's Punch Bowl waterfall. Somebody told Grant that this canyon was called the "Son-of-a B Canyon." It is reported that Grant's comment was, "You people sure know how to name things!"

In 1881, a stamp mill was built to crush the ore from the mines and a smelter was built to remove the gold from the ore. A wagon road from Gothic to Schofield had been constructed to bring in building materials and supplies. In the summer of 1882, the town had stores, mining companies, a boot and shoe maker, attorneys, a lumber mill, and a post office. The town had mail and stagecoach service to Gothic and Crested Butte. Since no rich ore was found in the mines of Schofield, the post office and the town shut down in 1885.

The first town north on the Schofield Pass road was Crystal City. Some of the Schofield miners moved to work there. They discovered crystal-form quartz in the mines of the valley and named their town Crystal. One of Colorado's famous photographs is the mill at the confluence of the North Fork and the South Fork of the Crystal River. The building was a hydro-electric plant producing compressed air and electricity for the mine's stamp mill and nearby mines.

The last town on the Schofield Pass road is named for the white rock discovered by George Yule in 1874. He found marble outcroppings along a creek later named Yule to honor him. The first claims to mine the marble were given to W. D. Parry, Sr., G. D. Griffith, and John McKay. They named their quarry "Yule."

In 1898, The Crystal River Railroad was built from the Denver and Rio Grande Railway at Carbondale to Redstone and Placita using standard gauge rails. The "Crystal River and San Juan Railway" then built south from Placita 7 1/3 miles into Marble and their first train ran on November 23, 1905. The Yule Quarry was in full operation in 1905 and 1906 with between 500 to 800 men working in the quarry and the finishing mill.

The first major contract for the Yule Marble Company was for the Lincoln Memorial in Washington, D.C. They built eighteen marble steps and thirty-six marble fluted columns to support the roof. The statue of Lincoln was sculpted from Georgia marble. The Memorial was dedicated on May 30, 1922.

The stone to mark the Tomb of the Unknown Soldier in Arlington National Cemetery also came from the Yule Quarry. The rough carving was done in Vermont, while the fine figures were carved after the stone was set at the cemetery. The three figures represent "victory, valor, and peace." The rear panel inscription is "Here rests in honored glory an American Soldier unknown but to God." The finished product was opened for public viewing on October 9, 1932.

The Schofield Pass Road ends at its junction with State Highway 133 at the base of the McClure Pass Road.

26
PEARL PASS

GPS Location: N 38° 58' 46" W 106° 49' 24"
Elevation: 12,705 feet
Road over top: September 1882
County: Gunnison/Pitkin
Gunnison/White River National Forest
Pass requires high clearance four wheel drive vehicle

In mid-1879, prospectors from Gunnison and Crested Butte crossed a divide on the pass named Pearl and discovered gold-bearing ore in Ashcroft south of Aspen. The town of Ashcroft was founded during the summer of 1881 with a population of 500 people. The town had stables, stores, saloons, a stage coach station, sporting houses, and a U.S. Post Office.

Pearl Pass was a historic crossing between the Aspen and Crested Butte Mining Districts. The pass was named for the Pearl Mine and Mountain, but nobody knew or would tell who Pearl was. The trail over Pearl was first built to be used by animals carrying ore. The animals used were either a male donkey, called a jackass, or a mule, the offspring of a male donkey and a female horse. A rope harness was used to align about thirty mules like railroad cars. They carried the ore on their backs from the mines to the mills and smelters. On their return trip they carried food, supplies, lumber, and mining tools.

In September of 1882, a wagon road was built on the Pearl Pass Trail. It was never a good road; in fact, it was only used for three years and then reverted to a jack trail in 1885. There are two reasons for the early demise of Pearl Pass. The first is that the pass's high elevation and heavy snow meant the road was open only in late summer and early fall. The other reason was the opening of roads nearby with lower pass elevations.

27
TAYLOR PASS

GPS Location: N 39° 01'13" W 106° 45' 20"
Elevation: 11,928 feet
First road over top: 1880
County: Gunnison/Pitkin
Gunnison/White River National Forest
Pass requires high clearance four wheel drive vehicle

Many prospectors were leaving the worked out mining camps of the Arkansas River Valley in the fall of 1878 to look for new mines that would produce more gold and silver. Some of them headed west out of today's town of Buena Vista to cross the Continental Divide using today's Cottonwood Pass. When they reached the west foot of the divide they were in today's Taylor Park. The park is about thirty miles long and ten miles wide and has a river flowing through it from the divide on the north end of the park.

Jim Taylor and Fred Lotis were pioneer prospectors in this new area. They had been told about the mines of Ashcroft over the divide on the north end of this park, and they enlisted other prospectors to help them build a trail. Many mines in the north end of Taylor Park produced high grade ore which brought in more prospectors. Two towns were built to provide housing, general stores, saloons, lumber mills, buildings for other services, and stables. The town of Bowman was built at the foot of the divide and became the major supply center for the north end of today's Taylor Park. Taylor

The Elk Mountain Range can be seen from the Taylor Pass road.

The summit of Taylor Pass is at the "V" in the center of the picture.

City was the first name of the other mining town. In 1900, that town was renamed Dorchester by the U.S. Postal Service when the post office was opened. The "Star" and the "Enterprise" Mines were the biggest producers of rich ore. The "Enterprise Mine and Mill" was electrified and produced silver ore until 1950.

In 1880, H. B. Gillespie's Stevens and Company built a wagon road over the divide to make it possible for wheeled vehicles to go from Taylor Park to Ashcroft and Aspen. The road from Taylor Park followed the Taylor River up to Taylor Lake and Taylor Pass. The earliest road over this pass required the teamsters to disassemble the wagons and lower them with rope down a steep embankment to a level area where the wagons were reassembled and continued the trip to Ashcroft. Gillespie built a narrow shelf road bypassing the steep embankment, and eliminating the need to disassemble the wagons and allowing them to safely travel downstream along Express Creek into Ashcroft. Stevens and Company started the first stagecoach company to operate between Bowman and Ashcroft.

This park, river, lake, creek, and pass road were officially named for the mining pioneer Jim Taylor in 1940 by the USGS Board on Geographic Names.

GUNNISON COUNTRY

28
KEBLER PASS

GPS Location: N 38° 50' 59" W 107° 06' 01"
Elevation: 9,980 feet
First road over top: 1893
County: Gunnison
Gunnison National Forest

The Kebler Pass road is today's Gunnison County Road 12. It starts at today's State Highway 133 just south of the Paonia Reservoir Dam. It heads east to cross Kebler Pass, then follows Coal Creek downstream into Crested Butte.

Kebler Pass and Road were named for John Kebler, an associate of John Charles Osgood who owned Colorado Fuel and Iron Company at Pueblo, Colorado. Kebler was also responsible for the coal mines which started the towns of Irwin, Ruby, Anthracite, and Floresta near Kebler Pass. Gold was discovered near Kebler Pass but not enough to mine. Coal was the main mineral of these mines. Two kinds of coal were mined, bituminous, called soft coal, and anthracite, called hard coal. The Denver and Rio Grande locomotives and the South Park engines preferred the hard coal because it would burn cleanly and hot.

The paved road on the right is the Kebler Pass road with its summit one mile ahead. The graveled road is the terminus of the Ohio Pass road.

GUNNISON COUNTRY

East Beckwith Mountain stands visible for miles along Kebler Pass road. In fall, Kebler Pass has some of the best color viewing in Colorado.

The Kebler Pass road west of the pass was part of a major Ute Indian trail used for migrating at the change of the seasons. When spring arrived, the Utes wintering in the San Luis Valley headed west across Cochetopa Pass into the Gunnison River Valley. The trail heads north from Gunnison to cross Ohio and Kebler Passes, then west along Ruby-Anthracite and Anthracite Creeks to the North Fork of the Gunnison River. The trail turns north and follows Muddy Creek to a divide and then follows Divide Creek down to the Colorado River. After crossing the river, the trail crosses the Roan Plateau to the White River Valley, then turns west to follow the White River into Utah.

The Crested Butte branch of the Denver and Rio Grande built a narrow gauge spur into the Kebler Pass area. It was built to haul coal into Crested Butte for the locomotives of the Denver and Rio Grande Railroad.

GUNNISON COUNTRY

29
OHIO PASS

GPS Location: N 38° 50' 05" W 107° 05' 30"
Elevation: 10,074 feet
First road over top: early 1880s
County: Gunnison
Gunnison National Forest

Ohio and Kebler Pass summits are about four miles apart, but are on separate ridges that divide several rivers and streams. Coming from the west settlers would follow Anthracite Creek upstream to cross Kebler Pass, then down along Coal Creek to today's Crested Butte. The Ohio Pass Road begins one mile south of Kebler Pass and follows Ohio Creek downstream to today's town of Gunnison.

The Ohio Creek headwaters are near today's Ohio Pass on the east side of Ohio Peak. The creek flows south through the valley guarded by the "Castles" to enter the Gunnison River. The first settlers on Ohio Creek were the Vidal Brothers, who

The Denver, South Park and Pacific railroad built a spur from Gunnison up the Ohio Creek Valley to Baldwin for coal. Shown here is part of the rail abutments at the townsite of Baldwin.

homesteaded in 1875 at the mouth of Ohio Creek. It is probable that the early settlers in this valley came from Ohio.

In the summer of 1876, the Crooke Brothers leased the Mt. Carbon Coal Mine. In order to be able to haul their coal to market, they built a wagon road to Gunnison, calling it the "Ohio Creek Toll Road." It was the only north/south road in the Ohio Creek Valley. The Mount Carbon coal deposits brought many people to work in their mines. The town of Castletown was built and incorporated on May of 1882 at the junction of Carbon and Ohio Creeks.

The Denver and South Park Railroad arrived in Gunnison in 1881. By 1883, the company had laid rails to Castleton and in late 1883 to Baldwin, the town closest to Ohio Pass. The South Park had graded their railway north over the pass and into the mining towns of Ruby and Irwin. To reach Ohio Pass the graders and rail builders duplicated the rock work they built for the Palisades west of the Alpine Tunnel. They built a wall of fitted stone blocks for proper grading for the rails. However, there is no evidence that the South Park laid rails beyond Baldwin.

Most of the coal mined at Baldwin was burned in South Park locomotives. The other coal mines in the Ohio Creek Valley shipped their coal to smelters in Gunnison. A few of the Ohio Valley's coal mines were still in operation after World War I.

The Castles are one of the interesting rock formations that can be seen from the Ohio Pass road.

GUNNISON COUNTRY

Mirror Lake is on the west side of the pass road midway between today's town of Tincup and the summit of Tincup Pass.

50
TINCUP PASS

GPS Location: N 38° 42' 55" W 106° 26' 04"
Elevation: 12,154 feet
First road over top: 1879
County: Chaffee/Gunnison
Gunnison/San Isabel National Forest
On the Continental Divide
Pass requires high clearance four wheel drive vehicle

When prospectors left the South Park mining camps, they crossed either Mosquito, Weston, or Trout Creek Pass to reach the Arkansas River Valley. From today's town of Nathrop many headed west upstream along the North Fork of Chalk Creek. They would pass the town of Alpine to reach St. Elmo, the starting point for several passes over the Continental Divide. They could go up Sawmill Hill to Tincup Pass on the Divide. They would go downhill on the west side of the divide to Mirror Lake and follow East Willow Creek to the new mining camps of the Tincup area.

We are told that the prospector named Fred Lottis walked into a mining camp with a tin cup of ore containing good "color." It is obvious that the miners chose to name their camp and town "Tin Cup." Placer mining in the nearby creeks was followed by hardrock mining, and by 1882 the Tin Cup mines were the largest producers of ore in Gunnison County.

The Chalk Creek and Elk Mountain Toll Road was incorporated on March 24, 1879. In late June a good wagon road was built over Tincup Pass and down into St. Elmo. In 1882 three stagecoach lines and "Witowski and Dunbar's Hack Line" were hauling people and ore over Tin Cup Pass. The Cumberland Pass road was built south out of Tincup to reach the Denver and South Park Railroad in Pitkin. The railroad could move the ore to smelters on the west side of the Continental Divide.

The town of Tincup survived the Silver Panic of 1893, but by the beginning of World War I, the town and pass road had died. Today the town is alive and well in the summer and fall months!

TOWNS OF VIRGINIA CITY AND TIN CUP

In 1878 a Denver banker named Edwin H. Hiller selected a townsite in the Willow Creek area of Taylor Park on the west side of the Continental Divide. When he returned in late March of 1879, the mining town of Virginia City had been incorporated on his site. He went two miles north and started the town of Hillerton on the east side of Willow Creek. The town grew quickly and it soon had cabins, a business district, and stables. Hillerton had the first bank and the first newspaper in Gunnison County. The mining camp called Abbeyville was built on the west side of Willow Creek across from Hillerton. It housed a mill, a smelter, and a few cabins.

Neither of the two mining camps described above could compete with Virginia City. It was located closest to the mines on the west side of the Continental Divide. Many residents of Hillerton and Abbeyville moved to live, love, and work in Tincup.

The mining town of Virginia City was started when rich ore was discovered at the Gold Cup and Tincup Mines in 1878. A group of investors led by Colonel L. I. Morris and A. J. Sparks Incorporated the town on March 2, 1879. A post office was started also using the name Virginia City. The U.S. Postal Service already had a Virginia City in both Nevada and Montana, so they renamed the town Tin Cup, which the citizens voted to accept by a vote of ninety-seven to three in an election in 1882. The town was incorporated with its new name.

Tin Cup started a "one room" school in 1881. A few years later the town changed the spelling of "Tin Cup" to "Tincup." The town grew to about 3,000 residents in 1882. Businesses included three hotels, two banks, a drygoods store, a bakery, two newspapers, three doctors, a lumberyard, butcher shops, grocery stores, and twenty-six saloons. One of the first saloons was opened by "Frenchy" Perrault, a Canadian. His saloon was a big tent with split logs for the bar and tables. It is reported that he had three barrels of liquor brought in for his grand opening. As in most mining towns, his large saloon was also used for church services and as a courthouse.

The most dangerous job in Tincup was that of the town marshal. From 1880 to 1883 seven men held the job. Three were shot and killed, one went insane, and only one served a full term.

Two major fires almost ended the town of Tincup. The first destroyed six businesses on August 22 in 1906. The second fire consumed ten businesses on May 31, 1913.

The ore from the Tincup Mining District was too complex for local smelters to handle. The ore contained sulfides, carbonates, and chlorides which held silver, gold, lead, and copper. The ore had to be shipped over the Divide to St. Elmo or over Cumberland Pass to the South Park Railroad at Pitkin adding extra costs to their finished product. If the ore could have been reduced locally, shipping costs would have been cut in half. The last attempted mining was dredging for gold in Willow Creek north of Tincup. From 1908 to 1917, two companies dredged and both lost money.

Tincup was the home of the legendary mail carrier Alex Parent. After he was injured from an explosion on West Gold Hill in Taylor Park, he carried mail for the U.S. Post Office. From 1880 to 1918 he carried the mail over the Divide between St. Elmo and Tincup, and also across Taylor Park to Dorchester. After his final crossing he served as the mayor of Tincup until his death in 1930.

Tincup is at the base of Tincup and Cottonwood Passes on the Continental Divide and Cumberland Pass into Pitkin.

31
CUMBERLAND PASS

GPS Location: N 38° 41' 21" W 106° 29' 03"
Elevation: 12,020 feet
First road over top: 1882
County: Gunnison
Gunnison National Forest

In 1880, prospectors headed south from the town of Tincup to cut a Jack-train trail over a divide 2½ miles west of the Continental Divide. In 1882, a good wagon road was built on this trail upstream along West Willow Creek to a wide open pass at the elevation of 12,220 feet. From the pass, the road was built downstream along North Quartz Creek to the town of Pitkin.

Ice Mountain and the Three Apostles can be seen from the north side of Cumberland Pass.

The name "Cumberland" was borrowed from a county in England. It was also used for a gap between Kentucky and Tennessee. This Colorado pass is named and the road is identified in a Rand McNally Map printed in 1888.

The Denver and South Park Railroad decided to build the first tunnel under the Continental Divide. The site chosen for the tunnel was above the towns of Hancock and Romley. Their route was underneath the Altman Pass trail. The Alpine Tunnel was bored through on December 21, 1881. In June of 1882, the first train ran through the tunnel and across the Palisades to the Sherrod Curve. From there the railroad followed Middle Quartz Creek downstream to its confluence with North Quartz Creek and the Cumberland Road two miles north of Pitkin.

The completion of the railroad brought more activity to the Cumberland Pass Road. Workers from the mining districts of Tincup and the mines on the Cumberland Road brought their ore to the railroad for transportation to Gunnison's smelters. Tincup is near the start of Tincup Pass on the west and Cottonwood Pass on the east side of the Divide and on the north end of the Cumberland Pass to Pitkin.

32
WAUNITA PASS

GPS Location: N 38° 34' 42" W 106° 30' 34"
Elevation: 10,260 feet
First road over top: 1880
County: Gunnison
Gunnison National Forest

The Ute Indians used the water of many Colorado hot springs for healing and maintenance of health. The creek now named "Hot Springs" starts on the west side of the Continental Divide and flows into the large natural hot water reservoir at today's Waunita Hot Springs.

The Ute Indians named the springs "Tomichi," their word for hot or boiling water. The Utes give us their story of a maiden named Waunita whose lover was a Shoshoni warrior. When he was killed in a raid, she died of a broken heart. The hot water rising from the ground where she was buried were her tears according to Ute legend.

The South Park Railroad came through the Alpine Tunnel down to the mining town of Pitkin in July, 1882, and into the town of Gunnison on September 2, 1882. Pitkin then became a large railroad town. A road was built out of Pitkin using the Indian trail over this low divide to reach the hot springs and the Tomichi Creek silver mines. Almost over night stagecoaches were carrying people to the hot springs and freighters were moving silver ore to Pitkin.

The first owner of the Hot Springs was Colonel R. S. Moore. He built a small bath house on the upper springs in 1879. During the summer of 1882, he built a two-story hotel with a bath house and called it the Hot Springs House. In 1882, Charles Elgin visited the springs. After using the waters he bought the lower springs and claimed that his rheumatism was cured. He built the "Elgin House" with eight private bath rooms. Soon the hot springs area became a major health resort.

In 1883, Elgin sold his property to Moore. Later, Moore sold the Waunita Hot Springs to Dr. Charles and Carolyn Davis. They upgraded the resort by building the three-story Waunita Hotel, a sanitarium, and a thirty by sixty foot swimming pool. In 1920, a fire damaged the hotel, sanitarium, and cabins, but Davis quickly remodeled the entire facility. When the Colorado State Geologist discovered radium in the hot springs water, Davis advertised that drinking and bathing in the water would cure rheumatism, arthritis, ulcers, tuberculosis, and tonsillitis. It is to his credit that by not allowing alcohol at the spa other problems were cured.

In 1962 the Pringle Family bought the hot springs resort. Since then they have created and operated a premier dude ranch with hot waters that are physically and spiritually healing.

TOWN OF PITKIN

Six prospectors set out from Lake City in the summer of 1878 headed north along the Lake Fork of the Gunnison River to its confluence with the Gunnison River. The men were named Frank Curtis, Wayne Scott, William and A.B. Campbell, Jed Watson, and William Jackson. From the confluence they went east to today's town of Parlin, where they headed north through the townsite of Ohio City to the townsite of Pitkin. They staked three good claims and returned to Lake City for the winter.

These men returned in 1879 to survey their new town and named it Quartzville. When they incorporated their town in 1880, they changed its name to Pitkin to honor Colorado's Governor Frederick W. Pitkin. As in all mining towns Pitkin was only a tent city at first. Three sawmills worked hard to provide the lumber for building stores and cabins. Supplies needed for this fast-growing mining town came over Cochetopa Pass from Saguache in the San Luis Valley. Supplies also came from the Arkansas River Valley to St. Elmo, and from there the freight wagons would cross the Continental Divide using the Denver, South Park and Pacific Alpine Pass Toll Road and follow Quartz Creek down to Pitkin.

The winter of 1880-1881 shut down this new mining town, but the spring of 1881 brought miners, stagecoaches, and freight wagons with supplies to build a permanent town.

During the first week of July, 1882, the South Park's construction train rolled through the Alpine Tunnel. On July 13, the South Park's first passenger train went through Pitkin, Ohio City, and Parlin. The South Park train entered Gunnison on August 8, 1882.

During the summer of 1882, Pitkin's silver veins were found to be shallow, the ore to be low-grade, and the miners moved on. Three major fires destroyed most of Pitkin's business district. They happened in October of 1883, November of 1898 and December of 1903. In 1913, a State Fish Hatchery was built south of town and is still in operation. Pitkin is not a ghost town; it is alive and well year around.

CONTINENTAL DIVIDE—CENTRAL COLORADO

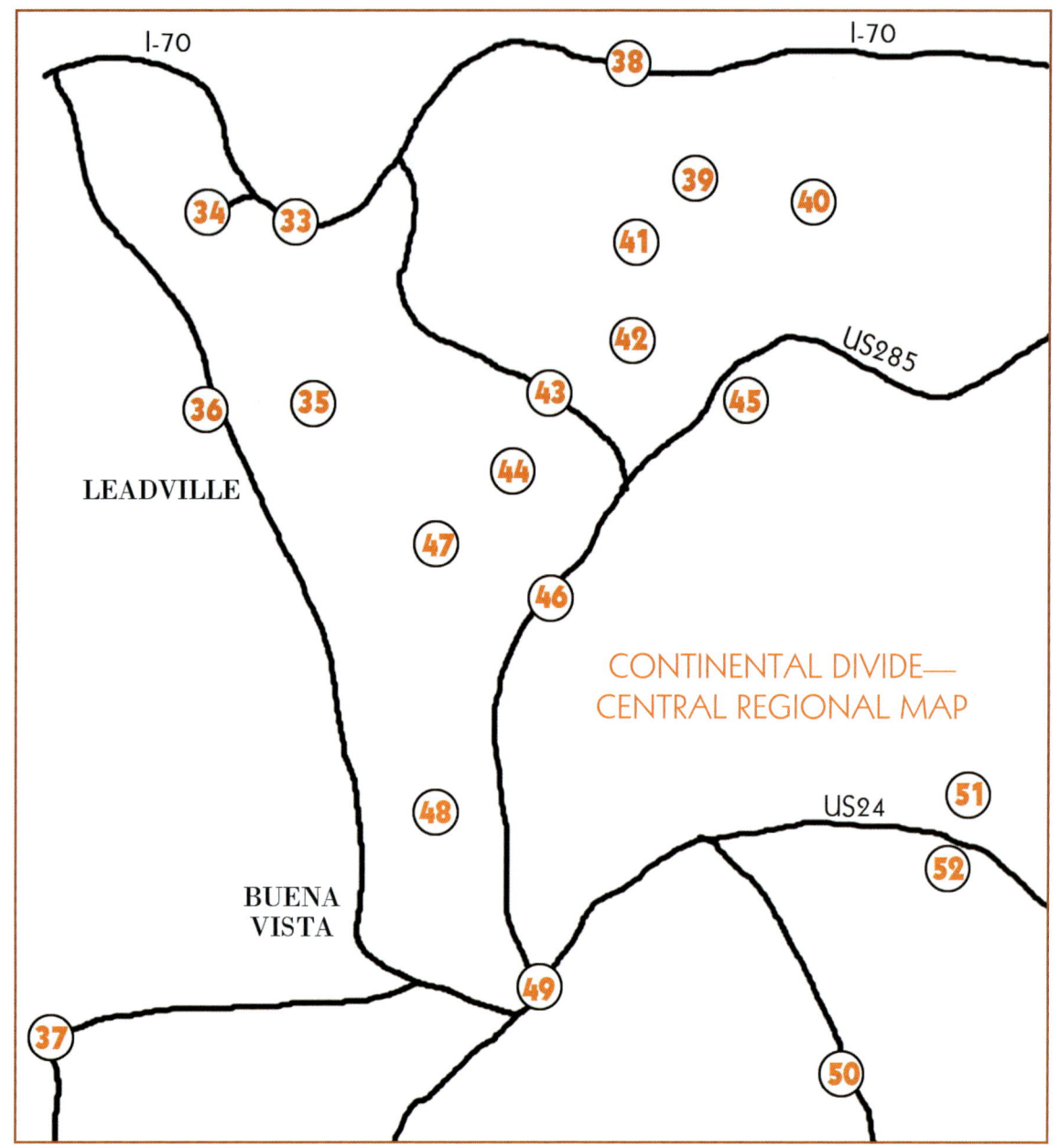

CONTINENTAL DIVIDE—CENTRAL REGIONAL MAP

33 Vail Pass
34 Shrine Pass
35 Fremont Pass
36 Tennessee Pass
Town of Leadville
37 Cottonwood Pass (On the Continental Divide)
38 Loveland Pass
39 Argentine Pass
40 Guanella Pass
Town of Georgetown
41 Webster Pass
42 Georgia Pass
43 Boreas Pass
Town of Breckenridge
44 Hoosier Pass
45 Kenosha Pass
46 Red Hill Pass
47 Mosquito Pass
48 Weston Pass
49 Trout Creek Pass
50 Currant Creek Pass
51 La Salle Pass
52 Wilkerson Pass

CONTINENTAL DIVIDE—CENTRAL COLORADO

33
VAIL PASS

GPS Location: N 39° 31' 50" W 106° 13' 02"
Elevation: 10,603 feet eastbound
10,662 feet westbound
First road over top: 1939
County: Eagle/Summit
Arapaho/White River National Forest

The east end of today's Vail Pass road starts at the junction of State Highway 91 and I-70, which was named Wheeler Junction. The Vail road runs upstream along West Ten Mile Creek and Corral Creek to the pass summit. From the top the road runs next to Black Lakes and continues downstream along Black Gore Creek through Vail, ending at Dowd's Junction.

Prior to the 1930s, the Ute Indians were the only humans crossing this pass trail. During road construction at the pass many pottery shards and hunting weapon points were dug from tent circles and fire rings indicating heavy use of a large campsite.

In the early 1930s Charles D. Vail resigned as Parks Manager of Denver to become the Chief Engineer of the Colorado Highway Department. In the mid-1930s, he upgraded Loveland's old wagon road over the Continental Divide by building U.S. 6 across Loveland Pass and down into Dillon. In the late 1930s, he built U.S. 6 along the side of Ten Mile Creek to Wheeler Junction. In 1939, U.S. 6 was built west up Ten Mile and Corral Creeks to the pass summit. Instead of using the old Shrine Pass Road, he built a new road down from the pass alongside Black Lakes and Black Gore Creek to the Eagle River. U.S. 6 was the first road built over Vail Pass. The pass road was named to honor Charles D. Vail in 1950 by the USGS Board on Geographic Names. The contractors of I-70 used the route of U.S. 6 to build the four-lane I-70 in the 1970s.

34
SHRINE PASS

GPS Location: N 39° 32' 50" W 106° 14' 32"
Elevation: 11,089 feet
First road over top: 1923
County: Eagle/Summit
Arapaho/White River National Forest

William Henry Jackson led the Hayden Surveyor's Photographic Unit to find the mountain with a cross in 1873. Stories had circulated about a peak in the Sawatch Range of the Rockies that had a snowy cross on its face. They found the mountain and

CONTINENTAL DIVIDE—CENTRAL COLORADO

Mount of the Holy Cross

set their camp on a nearby mountain for Jackson. On the morning of August 23, 1873, Jackson shot his most famous photograph. The cross is on the northeast face of Holy Cross Mountain, which is one of Colorado's 53 fourteeners. The cross is 1500 feet tall with the arms being 750 feet wide. The right arm of the cross has been shortened by a rockslide.

The Shrine Pass road starts at the top of Vail Pass and ends at the town of Red Cliff, the only town on the road. The town was started by prospectors in 1879. Cabins and stores were built, a mill site chosen, and a town company formed. A smelter was built and operated by the Battle Mountain Mining and Smelting Company. The Denver and Rio Grande Railroad graded and spiked down rails for their railway through Red Cliff along the Eagle River to Minturn and Dotsero. At Dotsero the Eagle River joins the Colorado River and the rails were laid into Glenwood Springs.

In 1923, the Shrine road was named the Holy Cross Trail. In 1950, the U.S.G.S. Board on Geographics named the road and pass "Shrine" because of its view of the Mount of the Holy Cross. For many years this road was part of the main route between Denver and Grand Junction.

35
FREMONT PASS

GPS Location: N 39° 21' 59" W 106° 11' 12"
Elevation: 11,318 feet
First road over top: Late 1870s
County: Lake
Public Access/On the Divide

This pass is six miles due north of Mosquito Pass as the eagle flies. It is named for Captain John Fremont who was sent by the United States Army Corps of Topographical Engineers to find passes through the Rockies for military use. Fremont crossed this area in June of 1844.

CONTINENTAL DIVIDE—CENTRAL COLORADO

Bartlett Mountain as seen from the west side of Fremont Pass.

Two narrow gauge railroads crossed the pass now named Fremont. In 1880 General William J. Palmer's Denver and Rio Grande Railroad built their Blue River Branch north out of Leadville over Fremont Pass to Wheeler Junction and through Ten Mile Canyon into old Dillon.

The second railroad to cross Fremont Pass was Dr. John Evan's Denver, South Park and Pacific in 1884. His rails headed north out of Como in South Park along Tarryall Creek to cross the Continental Divide on Boreas Pass. From the pass the rails followed Indiana Creek into Frisco. The rails then headed south through Ten Mile Canyon past Copper Mountain to Fremont Pass. From the pass they followed the East Fork of the Arkansas River fourteen miles into Leadville.

Unusual ore was discovered on this pass on the western slope of Bartlett Mountain in 1879. A solo prospector named Charles Senter found a strange yellow colored mineral while looking for gold. When he broke it up, he found a gray mineral with veins of a darker material that he thought was graphite. He sent samples of this material to the Colorado School of Mines at Golden in 1893. In 1895, the mineral was correctly identified as "molybdenum disulfide or molybdenite" by Professor Rudolph George at the School of Mines.

In 1916, Max Scott formed the Climax Molybdenite Company to mine and process this metal. The chromium group metal was mixed with carbon to harden steel. At first it was used as a substitute for tungsten. It was discovered that its best use was to strengthen steel used to make armor plating and large gun barrels during World War I. Later "Moly" was used for the turbines of jet engines and stainless steel products. The Climax Mine is thirteen miles north of Leadville.

CONTINENTAL DIVIDE—CENTRAL COLORADO

36
TENNESSEE PASS

GPS Location: N 39° 19' 17" W 106° 18' 40"
Elevation: 10,424 feet
First road over top: 1879
County: Eagle/Lake
San Isabel/White River National Forest

The buffalo and the Ute Indians were the first mammals to use this gentle pass over the Continental Divide from the Eagle River headwaters to the headwaters of the East Fork of the Arkansas River. The Arkansas River runs south near today's towns of Leadville, Granite, Buena Vista, Nathrop, and is joined by the South Arkansas River in today's Salida.

This pass was used by fur trappers and traders in the early 1830s. Captain John Fremont crossed this pass on his trip to California in 1845. In 1873, the Hayden surveyors led by Dr. Hayden and his topographer Archibald Marvine crossed Tennessee to find the Mount of the Holy Cross and continue measuring and mapping Western Colorado. In 1879, a good wagon road was built from Leadville over the Divide to today's town of Red Cliff. The pass was probably named by prospectors from Tennessee.

The Denver and Rio Grande Railroad started to lay rails north from today's town of Salida in the spring of 1880. They followed the Arkansas River through Buena Vista and Granite to build into Leadville in the summer of 1880. They laid rails north out of Leadville in 1881 to cross the summit of Tennessee Pass at an elevation of 10,324 feet. Rails were laid in the Eagle River Valley to Red Cliff, Gilman, and Minturn. From Minturn, they built rails west to run alongside the Colorado River through Glenwood Canyon into Glenwood Springs on October 5, 1887.

On November 30, 1888, a survey was completed for a tunnel to be bored under Tennessee Pass at the elevation of 10,221 feet. Work was started in 1889 and the tunnel was bored through in 1890. The railroad started using the tunnel on November 20, 1891.

The U.S. Army opened Camp Hale in 1942 in the Upper Eagle River Valley, north of Tennessee Pass. The new soldiers were brought here to train for winter and mountain combat using skis, new weapons, and munitions. They served in the Tenth Mountain Division, the 38th Regimental Combat Team, and the 99th Infantry Battalion. Ski training was on the north side of the Continental Divide at "Ski Cooper." The men fought in Europe and in Italy to help end World War II. In 1964, Camp Hale was dismantled and the land deeded to the U.S. Forest Service.

CONTINENTAL DIVIDE—CENTRAL COLORADO

TOWN OF LEADVILLE

The first mineral discovered in Leadville was gold at California Gulch in 1860. Prospectors from the East entered South Park over Kenosha Pass or Wilkerson Pass. After crossing South Park, they could use Mosquito, Weston, or Trout Creek Passes to reach the Arkansas River Valley and Leadville.

The silver mining boom at Oro City (Oro is Spanish for gold) in California Gulch rocked the mining world in 1878 with the news that the silver boom at Leadville could be richer than Central City and Georgetown's silver booms. The value of the silver produced at Oro City went from $26,000 in the late 1870s to $11.5 million in 1880.

William Stevens and Alvinus Woods, metallurgists and mining engineers, were the first to recognize the value of the black sands that clogged up their sluice boxes during placer mining for gold. The black sand was a carbonate of lead heavily laced with veins of silver.

A merchant named H.A.W. Tabor opened a mining town on the north side of Oro City that he called "Slabtown." In August of 1868, the future Leadville had six businesses: two general stores, one saloon, one boardinghouse, a drugstore, and a wagon shop. By 1878, the town of Leadville was incorporated with a city council, mayor, city marshal, and a post office.

H.A.W. Tabor owned a general store and was willing to "grubstake" men wanting to be prospectors. He sold them supplies on credit in return for part ownership of their mines and silver-bearing ore. He grubstaked August Rische and George Hawk who discovered the rich "Little Pittsburg Mine" in 1878. Tabor sold his third of the mine for one million dollars and with that money became Leadville's richest citizen.

By the end of 1879, Leadville's population was about 10,000 people with that many more living in the camps around the town. A toll road was built from Fairplay up North Mosquito Gulch to the Mosquito Pass summit and down to California Gulch and Leadville in the spring of 1879. Mosquito Pass, at its elevation of 13,186 feet, is the highest road pass in Colorado.

Three of Colorado's first railroads were built into Leadville. Palmer's Denver and Rio Grande entered Salida on May 20, 1880. It headed north up the Arkansas River Valley to enter Leadville in late July. Dr. John Evan's Denver, South Park and Pacific railroad was built north out of Como to cross the Continental Divide over Boreas Pass. Rails were laid along Indiana Creek into Breckenridge and along the Blue River to Frisco and Ten Mile Creek to Wheeler Junction. Heading south, the South Park Railway crossed the Continental Divide on Fremont Pass and continued downstream along the east fork of the Arkansas River into Leadville in 1884. William J. Hagerman's standard gauge "Midland Railroad" started construction in Colorado Springs. His railway was built west over Ute Pass and across South Park to Trout Creek Pass. Next, the rails were built along Trout Creek down into the Arkansas River Valley. From there, the rails were laid north through today's Buena Vista and Granite, and arrived in Leadville in the summer of 1887.

CONTINENTAL DIVIDE—CENTRAL COLORADO

Near the summit of Cottonwood Pass, the road headed west becomes a winding dirt and graveled road down into Taylor Park.

37
COTTONWOOD PASS
(ON THE CONTINENTAL DIVIDE)

GPS Location: N 38° 49' 40" W 106° 24' 33"
Elevation: 12,126 feet
First road over top: Early 1877
County: Chaffee/Gunnison
San Isabel/Gunnison National Forest
On the Continental Divide

The Sawatch Mountain Range runs north and south parallel to the Continental Divide. This range is the west shoulder of the Arkansas River Valley. The range begins at the Eagle River on the North and ends at Monarch Pass on the south. Some of the Sawatch Mountains are called the Collegiates. Their names are Oxford, Harvard, Columbia, Yale, and Princeton, and they are all "fourteeners."

The Cottonwood Pass road headed west out of today's Buena Vista follows an old Indian trail upstream along Cottonwood Creek in the gap between Mt. Yale and Mt. Princeton. The road follows the North Fork of Cottonwood Creek for seventeen miles to the wide opening of Cottonwood Pass on the Continental Divide. From the top of the divide, the road runs down through today's Taylor Park to the Taylor River, and then south through Almont to the city named Gunnison.

CONTINENTAL DIVIDE—CENTRAL COLORADO

Just west of the summit, the Cottonwood Pass becomes a dirt road which turns into a section of curves and hairpin turns.

The freighter Dave Wood bought the Cottonwood Pass road and improved it to a wagon road in 1877. He wanted to haul freight from Colorado Springs to the new mining districts in the San Juan Mountains. By 1881, he was the largest freighter on the Western Slope. He dominated the freighting business in the San Juan, Uncompahgre, and Gunnison country. Two major events crippled his business. The first was the arrival of the Denver and Rio Grande Railroad into Gunnison in 1881. The second was the "Silver Panic" of 1893. The U.S. Government stopped buying silver as promised, the mines closed, and thousands of miners were out of work. When Dave was asked, "Do you know anything about the mountains?" by a potential customer, he answered, "I hauled these mountains in here!" Frances and Dorothy Wood used his reply for the title of his auto-biography that they published in 1977.

In 1960, the U.S. Forest Service rebuilt the Cottonwood Pass Road for four-wheel drive vehicles on both sides of the Continental Divide. This road was the most direct route from Buena Vista to Gunnison. Today there is a Forest Service sign near the top of the pass identifying the "Meadows Stage Stop." There was a stage stop here from 1883 to 1901 to give passengers and horses a pit stop.

CONTINENTAL DIVIDE—CENTRAL COLORADO

The Front Range as seen from the summit of Loveland Pass.

38
LOVELAND PASS

GPS Location: N 39° 39' 49" W 105° 52' 45"
Elevation: 11,990 feet
First road over top: February, 1879
County: Clear Creek/Summit
Arapaho National Forest
On the Continental Divide

William A. H. Loveland was born and raised in Massachusetts. He fought in the Civil War and came west for California's gold rush. He arrived in Golden in 1859 with a wagon full of supplies to open a general store. He heard about Leadville's gold rush and decided to build a road up Clear Creek to cross the Continental Divide to reach the western slope's goldfields. He organized the Bakerville and Leadville Wagon Road Company to build his high line wagon road in 1878. He started work on the road in the winter of 1887 with 100 men, horses, wagons, scrapers, dynamite, and a chuck-wagon. The road was built to the top of the pass in February of 1879 and completed to the bottom of the Snake River in May of 1879. A freight line started crossing the pass in late May and S.W. Notts' Georgetown and Leadville Stage started daily service to Leadville.

Loveland knew that the success of Golden depended upon a railroad through the Rockies. He enlisted the Civil Engineer Edward Louis Berthoud to find a Continental Divide Pass for a railroad. Berthoud hired the mountain man Jim Bridger to help him and together they located the divide crossing we call Berthoud Pass today.

Loveland incorporated the Colorado and Clear Creek Railroad Company in 1865. He named his railroad the Colorado Central Railroad and started laying rails from

CONTINENTAL DIVIDE—CENTRAL COLORADO

Golden to Denver in 1868. He received support from the Union Pacific to lay his narrow gauge rails up Clear Creek to Idaho Springs and up North Clear Creek almost to Central City. The railroad continued through Idaho Springs to reach Georgetown in 1877. The railroad climbed the Georgetown Loop to reach Silver Plume and its terminus in Graymount.

The Colorado State Highway Commission used Loveland's wagon road to build U.S. 6 over the Continental Divide. It was opened for traffic on August 20, 1932.

39
ARGENTINE PASS

GPS Location: N 39° 37' 31" W 105° 46' 57"
Elevation: 13,207 Feet
First road over top: 1869
County: Clear Creek/Summit
Forest Service: Arapaho
On the Continental Divide
No road over top today

In 1873 the Hayden Surveyors located and recorded a new pass on the Continental Divide in today's Clear Creek County. The pass made traveling possible from the Clear Creek Valley on the east side of the Divide over to the Snake River Valley on the west side. They measured its altitude at 13,132 feet, but today's topo maps show its altitude at 13,207 feet. The name of Argentine, Latin for "silver," was first given to the rich silver discoveries on the east side of the Divide, then to the pass and the mining district on the west side of the Divide.

In 1868 miners from Georgetown and Silver Plume bought a charter to build a toll road to the pass. There is no record or evidence that this group attempted to actually build this road.

In June of 1867, Stephen Decatur organized his Georgetown and Snake River Wagon Road Company to build over Argentine Pass. The Georgetown newspaper reported that in June of 1867 Decatur had surveyed and staked the beginning of his "Georgetown Argentine and Silveropilis Wagon Road." His road builders started in Georgetown headed west up along Leavenworth Creek to the East Argentine Mining District and to the top of the pass during the summer of 1868. In the summer of 1869 he built his road west across the side of Ruby Mountain to the headwaters of Peru Creek. From there the road went downstream along the Snake River to the towns of Montezuma and Dillon. Decatur's road was completed on October 21, 1869.

Because of its high altitude, Argentine Pass was often blocked by deep snow each winter from mid-September to mid-July. Because of high maintenance costs and low revenue from the toll charges, the road company stopped using the road. After that the road was only used for jack trains, but that was short lived also.

CONTINENTAL DIVIDE—CENTRAL COLORADO

Excerpts from the original Georgetown and Argentine Wagon Road Charter

CONTINENTAL DIVIDE—CENTRAL COLORADO

THE ARGENTINE CENTRAL RAILROAD

It is not known who gave the name of Argentine to the pass, the mining districts, and the railroad built to serve the many mines on the east side of the pass. George Griffith and his brother did not "strike it rich" while prospecting at Central City and chose to move to the area of the town to be named later after George. On September 14, 1864, James Huff and two friends made their strike of "Argentiferous" rock containing silver ore. Many other miners helped to make the Georgetown-Silver Plume Region the largest silver producing area in Colorado at the time.

Edward J. Wilcox's first job in the Georgetown area was sorting ore in the Cashier Mine near Webster Pass. He bought his first claim near the Excelsior Lode. During the winters of 1881-1883, he was a student of the Colorado School of Mines at Golden. Later he entered the Methodist Ministry and served front range parishes until 1892.

When he returned to mining, he bought several profitable claims at Idaho Springs and in the East Argentine District south of Silver Plume. He continued buying and selling claims until he owned sixty-five mining properties. In July of 1902 he formed the Waldorf Mining and Milling Company which operated at the head of Leavenworth Gulch, nine miles south of Silver Plume.

Because of the difficulty of using wagons and pack animals to move ore from the mines to the smelters, Wilcox decided to build his own railroad. With ground breaking on August 1, 1905, the Argentine Central Railroad started construction at the Colorado and Southern Railhead in Silver Plume. He used three-foot-wide rails for a narrow gauge train because the narrow gauge "Shay Locomotive" could climb grades of ten to fourteen percent and make tighter switchback curves. His crews built nine miles of rails over a mountain in four months time, reaching the Wilcox Mining Tunnel on January 31, 1906. A Golden Spike Ceremony was held at the mine portal in the town named Waldorf.

From Waldorf the construction crew started laying rails that went to the top of Mount McClellan. One year to the day after the start of the construction the route was completed to the top of Mt. McClellan.

This narrow gauge line from Silver Plume to the top of Mt. McClellan was the only traction railroad in the world of comparable height outside of the Andes. Its 4,500 feet climb from about 9,100 feet to 13,644 feet was accomplished on tracks about sixteen miles long with an average grade of 5 1/3 percent.

The first carload of ore was shipped from Waldorf over the Argentine Central Rails to Silver Plume on February 13, 1906. By mid-summer about fifty tons of ore a day was shipped from the Waldorf mill to Silver Plume. Tourism was the second top money producer for the Argentine Central. The first passenger trip to the top of Mt. McClellan was made on August 1, 1906. The view from the top of the Rockies was something that most tourists had never seen. The two fourteeners, Gray's and Torrey's Peaks, were just a mile west of Mt. McClellan. It was Wilcox's decision not to run the trains on Sunday, not so strange when you remember that he was a former minister.

As early as 1893, aerial transportation was used to access roadless mining districts. The idea for a passenger tramway above Silver Plume was started with a survey for a line in 1903. The tram ran south from near the Railroad Pavilion in Silver Plume to the top of a peak on Leavenworth Mountain which they named "Sunrise Peak." The

CONTINENTAL DIVIDE—CENTRAL COLORADO

tram was incorporated for the Colorado Mines and Aerial Tramway Company on April 27, 1906. Construction was started on May 19, 1906. After some delays in construction, the first ride to the top was on August 12, 1907. The elevation gain from bottom to top was about 3,000 feet and it took forty minutes for a round trip. It provided the Clear Creek area with its third tourist attraction besides the train ride on the Georgetown Loop and the Mt. McClellan train ride.

40
GUANELLA PASS

GPS Location: N 39° 35' 42" W 105° 42' 40"
Elevation: 11,669 feet
First road over top: summer 1955
County: Clear Creek
Arapaho National Forest

The first men to cross this pass from the Clear Creek Valley into South Park were prospectors looking for silver and gold.

In March of 1860, a Swiss civil engineer named Edward Berthoud arrived in Golden to live and work. He was hired by William A. H. Loveland to hunt for good pass crossings over the Continental Divide that could be used by vehicles and railroads. Berthoud hired Jim Bridger, who was described as a "topographical genius" because of his work for the millionaire fur trader Ashley and other traders, to be his guide.

In May of 1861 Berthoud sent Jim Bridger and his crew south out of Georgetown to cross today's Guanella Pass and head down to today's town of Grant. From there they headed southwest over Kenosha Pass into South Park to examine Georgia Pass and Boreas Pass for possible use as stagecoach and railroad routes to California.

Meanwhile, Berthoud and two helpers went north from Georgetown to the town of Empire. They headed west up the West Fork of Clear Creek to look at Jones Pass and Vasquez Pass as possible Continental Divide crossings. They found an unnamed pass east of the other two passes and chose it as the best railroad route. It is the pass that we now call Berthoud Pass.

In the fall and winter of 1873, the English Lady Isabella L. Bird toured the Colorado Rockies. She liked to travel alone and on horseback. Part of the time, she was guided by her guide and companion named "Mountain Jim." Her diary of this trip is written as letters to her sister Henrietta in England and is published in her book *A Lady's Life in the Rocky Mountains*. While in Golden she said that she wanted to see Green Lake above Georgetown. She used a two and a half mile trail up the future Guanella Pass road. From the elevation of almost 12,000 feet she could see that Green Lake was covered with ice. She returned to Georgetown after dark.

Another story that needs to be told is about a project built along South Clear Creek and the Guanella Pass Road. When the Cabin Creek hydroelectric plant went online next to this pass road, the Cabin Creek pump and storage installation was built at the

CONTINENTAL DIVIDE—CENTRAL COLORADO

From the Guanella Pass road, you are looking at Sawtooth Mountain on the left and Mount Bierstadt on the right.

highest elevation in the world for this type of hydroelectric plant. The plant works like a storage battery in an automobile's electrical system by using two water reservoirs, the upper located at the elevation of 11,202 feet. The plant is connected to a Denver power plant to help provide electricity for Denver. When electrical power is needed in Denver, water is released from the upper reservoir to the plant at the lower reservoir to generate and transmit electricity. When there is no demand from Denver, the generating plant's dual purpose reversible generator motors moves the water back to fill the upper reservoir for later use. The Public Service Company was recycling before a lot of us understood the concept.

This twenty mile long pass road from Georgetown to Grant was named to honor Byron Guanella, a Clear Creek County Commissioner, who worked long and hard for the completion of the Guanella Pass Road. His family states that it was dedicated and opened in the summer of 1955.

CONTINENTAL DIVIDE—CENTRAL COLORADO

TOWN OF GEORGETOWN

Kentuckians George and David Griffith arrived in today's Denver area in 1859. When the "gold rush" brought hundreds of prospectors to the Central City area to pan for gold, the Griffith brothers moved upstream on the South Fork of Clear Creek to build a cabin and look for gold. They chose to locate at today's site of Georgetown. George discovered the lode he named Griffith and worked the gold bearing quartz. Soon other family members arrived and many prospectors built cabins at "George's" town. The Griffith brothers built a toll road from Georgetown over the mountains into Central City. They used the road to haul machinery to build a stamp mill for crushing their ore.

The Griffith Mining Camp slowly grew into a town. The Griffith's mill was built and in operation in August of 1861. Settlers from the east came to find work and homes after the massive destruction created by the "Civil War." They came to build cabins, stores, stables, boarding houses, schools, and churches. In 1865, a new village was started next to Georgetown by William M. Hale. He named it Elizabethtown to honor his wife. On October 24, 1866, residents of both towns met to unite the two towns and call their town Georgetown. Georgetown was granted a post office in 1866 and chosen to be the county seat for the newly established Clear Creek County. The town had worked for and earned the name "Silver Queen."

Robert Steele, James Huff, and Robert Taylor discovered the rich silver ore of the Gus Belmont Lode at the top of Mt. McCllelan in mid-September of 1864. Choosing six other partners, they pooled their capital to obtain materials and supplies to form a mining district. They surveyed and staked claims to define and organize the "Argentine Mining District" on October 1, 1864. They started by locating three lode claims, the Gus Belmont, Nominee, and Halifax, and divided the area into two regions separated by the Continental Divide named East Argentine and West Argentine. The Argentine strike was Colorado's first major silver strike. Argentine is English for the Latin word Argentum translated silver.

In 1866 William A. Hamill moved his family from Central City to Georgetown. With hard work and careful business transactions, he became a wealthy man. In 1874 he bought a fine house where he and his wife raised their four sons and one daughter. He was an active civic leader and a generous citizen. He gave bells to the fire department and for the steeples of the Catholic and Episcopal Churches. In 1876 he was elected to the Colorado State Senate. Today the Hamill House is one of Georgetown's museums, along with the "Hotel De Paris" and the "Georgetown Energy Museum."

Georgetown is the starting point for the Guanella Pass Road over to the town of Grant on today's U.S. 285. Georgetown is also on the Loveland Pass Road that crosses the Continental Divide to reach Dillon and Silverthorne.

CONTINENTAL DIVIDE—CENTRAL COLORADO

41
WEBSTER PASS

GPS Location: N 39° 31' 50" W 105° 49' 58"
Elevation: 12,096 feet
First road over top: 1878
County: Park/Summit
Arapaho/Pike National Forest
On the Continental Divide
Pass requires high clearance four wheel drive vehicle

In the 1860s, two Norwegian prospectors from Cañon City headed west from today's town of Webster to cross the Continental Divide. Since they did not own a mule, they hitched themselves to a handcart full of supplies. They followed the North Fork of the South Platte River in the Hall Valley to a junction, a gulch that they used to reach the summit of the Continental Divide. A nearby mountain and their gulch are named "Handcart."

Emerson and William Webster were pioneers of the Snake River Mining District. They built a wagon road on the west side of the Continental Divide up to the divide's summit for the Montezuma Silver Mining Company. They changed the pass's name from Handcart to Webster, and continued their wagon road downstream along the North Fork of the South Platte River in Hall's Valley to today's town of Webster.

The Colorado Miner newspaper reported that the Snake River and Hall Valley road was completed in 1878. The road over the Divide is now named the Webster Pass Road.

Red Cone can be seen from the summit of Webster Pass. The pass road continues to the left of Red Cone to Grant.

CONTINENTAL DIVIDE—CENTRAL COLORADO

Mt. Gayot stands out at the summit of Georgia Pass.

42
GEORGIA PASS

GPS Location: N 39° 27' 31" W 105° 55' 00"
Elevation: 11,585 feet
First road over Top: early 1860s
County: Park/Summit
Arapaho/Pike National Forest
On the Continental Divide
Pass requires high clearance four wheel drive vehicle

Georgia Pass is four miles northeast of Boreas Pass on the Continental Divide. The Continental Divide was the boundary line of the early Kansas and Utah Territories from which the Colorado Territory was created.

On his return trip from California, Captain John Fremont followed a trail upstream along the Swan River. He did not cross Georgia Pass because Arapaho Indians were camping on it. Both the Ute and the Arapaho used this high crossing between South Park and the Blue River Valley.

Prospectors and trappers used Georgia Pass after the Civil War. It is probable that these early miners were from Georgia and named the pass to honor their state. When gold was discovered at Breckinridge, miners swarmed over the divide to go down the Swan River and widened the road for wagons. A charter for a toll road over Georgia Pass was granted in November of 1861. When the Hayden surveyors mapped this area in 1873, they noted that an established wagon road crossed Georgia Pass and was in good condition.

CONTINENTAL DIVIDE—CENTRAL COLORADO

In January of 1861, the *Rocky Mountain News* owner and editor reported that a Mr. Buford took eight wagons over Georgia Pass with the help of twenty men shoveling snow to clear the road.

43
BOREAS PASS

GPS Location: N 39° 24' 40" W 105° 58' 10"
Elevation: 11,481 feet
First road over top: 1860s
County: Park/Summit
White River/Pike National Forest
On the Continental Divide

The first name used for this Continental Divide Pass was "Ute." The first people to cross the pass were the Northern Utes headed south to winter in South Park and the San Luis Valley. "Tarryall" was the second name used, which was the name of a mining town on the east side of the Divide. "Breckenridge" was its next name, the name of the town on the west side of the divide. The Denver and South Park Railroad named the pass "Boreas," after the God of the North in Greek mythology, for the severe winds blowing across the pass. The mining boom in Breckenridge brought thousands of prospectors and miners across Boreas Pass in the early 1860s. The pass trail was widened into a good wagon road for freighters and stagecoaches to move materials and people over the Continental Divide.

Originally built in 1881 by Italian stonemasons, the six-bay Como Roundhouse was enlarged by adding eight wooden bays in the 1890s. In 1918, five of the wooden bays were removed.

In October of 1872, Dr. John Evans started building the narrow gauge railway named the Denver, South Park and Pacific out of Denver. He reached Morrison in June of 1874 where he ran out of money and steam. Five years later Evans started construction again, pushing the South Park up the South Platte Canyon and reaching Kenosha Pass in May of 1879. In late June the rails were spiked down to the Como townsite. Evans built a railroad town with a stone roundhouse; machine and blacksmith shops; a depot that housed a ticket office; waiting room and baggage room; and siding rails for car storage and for car passings. The railroad yard also included a water tower and wood and coal storage buildings. Evans also built housing and general stores for the railroad employees. The name Como referred to Lake Como in Italy.

Once again Evans needed financial help to be able to build the railway over Boreas Pass to Breckinridge and finally into Leadville. In 1882, Sidney Dillon, the president of the Union Pacific Railroad, built South Park's rails over Boreas Pass and over Fremont Pass into Leadville. The South Park Railroad was now able to carry ore and mining materials from Leadville to Denver.

The story is told that the P. T. Barnum Circus train, traveling from Denver to Leadville, couldn't make it up the Boreas Pass grade. The railroad men solved the problem by removing the elephants to lighten the weight in the boxcars. Next they used the elephants to pull and push the train up to the pass so that "The Greatest Show on Earth" could arrive in Leadville.

THE TOWN OF BRECKENRIDGE

Prospectors from South Park were the first to pan for gold in the Blue River Valley. They staked off claims just north of today's town of Breckenridge in August, 1859. General George Spencer platted a townsite and made the necessary improvements to homestead his property. In order to obtain a post office, he named the town Breckinridge, for John C. Breckinridge the Vice President of the United States from 1857 to 1861. General Spencer's reward was not only the post office, but also the postmaster's job. After Breckinridge lost his presidential election bid to Abraham Lincoln, he joined the Confederate Army. Angry pro-union town citizens wanted to change the name of their town, and they finally settled for changing the "I" to an "E" in Breckenridge.

Dredge boat by Cindy Williams.

CONTINENTAL DIVIDE—CENTRAL COLORADO

From 1859 to 1862, prospectors used three Continental Divide passes to get to Breckenridge and the Blue River Valley. From the town of Jefferson they crossed Georgia Pass, from Como they used Boreas Pass, and from the Alma/Fairplay towns they used Hoosier Pass.

The use of dredges to remove gold from the Blue and Swan Rivers brought a different method of mining to Breckenridge. The boats dredged up glacial rocks to remove from them the gravels and sands that contained gold. The dredges floated on ponds they made while dredging the river beds by digging up to fifty feet deep in a 200 foot corridor.

Father John Dyer was appointed as minister in the Blue River District of the Methodist Church in 1862. In 1880, he and his parishioners built the First Methodist Church west of the Continental Divide in Breckenridge on a lot next to the courthouse. The vestibule, steeple, and stained glass windows were added in 1889. In response to a minister's sermon against open saloons on Sunday, some miner set off dynamite in the belfry. The building was repaired and Father Dyer's church is still in business today.

44
HOOSIER PASS

GPS Location: N 39° 21' 42" W 106° 03' 45"
Elevation: 11,541 feet
First road over top: 1862
County: Park/Summit
Pike/Arapaho National Forest

The Hoosier Pass road starts at today's town of Alma, north of the town of Fairplay. It follows the Middle Fork of the South Platte River upstream to the pass summit. After crossing the pass the road continues north downstream along the Blue River into Breckenridge.

This photograph shot from the Hoosier Pass road shows fourteeners from Mount Lincoln to Quandry Peak.

CONTINENTAL DIVIDE—CENTRAL COLORADO

The first mammals to cross the Continental Divide over Hoosier Pass were the buffalo, and the Ute Indians were next to cross. They were following their food supply from Middle Park to South Park for their winter meat. The fur trader Rufus Sage crossed here in 1842.

In 1844, Lt. John Fremont's expedition, with Kit Carson and Tom Fitzpatrick as his guides, entered today's North Park and headed for Muddy Pass and South Park. In June of 1844, Fremont stood on Hoosier Pass. He noticed a stream which he correctly identified as the headwater of the South Platte River.

The pass was named for Hoosier Gulch which was being worked by prospectors from Indiana in the early 1860s. "Hoosier" is a nickname for residents of Indiana.

In 1862, The Empire City, New Pass and Montgomery City Road Company planned and built a road south over Hoosier Pass to the mining town of Montgomery. Other projects of this company were at the town of Empire and at Loveland Pass.

45
KENOSHA PASS

GPS Location: N 39° 24' 48" W 105° 45' 24"
Elevation: 10,001 feet
First road Over Top: 1862
County: Park
Pike National Forest

Kenosha Pass is crossed by today's U.S. 285 between the early gold rush mining towns of Grant on the north side and Jefferson on the south. It is reported that the pass is named for an early stagecoach driver from Kenosha, Wisconsin. Kenosha is said to be the Chippewa Indian word for pike fish. The first name of the pass was Kenosha Summit. The pass is the northern entry into South Park.

Zebulon Pike crossed here as well as trappers, mountain men, and fur traders. In 1859, prospectors were crossing to reach the goldfields of Fairplay, Alma, and the other mining camps on the east side of the Mosquito Mountain Range. Concord stagecoaches had regular routes over the pass by 1862 carrying mail, passengers, and freight. In 1864, the Kenosha House on the west side of the pass was a stage stop for changing horses and picking up customers.

In the mid-1870s the Denver, South Park and Pacific Railroad laid narrow gauge rails up along the North Fork of the South Platte River from Denver to Kenosha Pass. Their locomotives arrived at Kenosha on May 19, 1879. About fourteen miles southeast of the pass the South Park Railroad construction crews built a town with a railroad station that was named Como.

The South Park went two directions from Como. Rails were laid north over Boreas Pass through today's town of Breckenridge, then on to today's town of Frisco. From there the rails followed Ten Mile Creek south through Wheeler Junction and then climbed to cross the Continental Divide. The South Park's main route headed south

CONTINENTAL DIVIDE—CENTRAL COLORADO

out of Como to cross Trout Creek Pass into the Arkansas River Valley. Crossing the river, rails were laid south to today's town of Nathrop. From there they headed west to St. Elmo and Hancock at the foot of the Continental Divide. The Alpine Tunnel was bored through the mountains and rails were built down to Pitkin, Ohio City, Parlin, and Gunnison.

46
RED HILL PASS

GPS Location: N 39° 16' 04" W 105° 57' 40"
Elevation: 9,993 feet
First road over top: 1861
County: Park
Public assess through private land

The road over Red Hill Pass is today's U.S. 285. The pass is named for the red hill two miles south of the pass crossing. The pass is located halfway between Como and Fairplay, near the middle of South Park.

In 1859, settlers crossed the pass to reach the headwaters of the South Platte River. The pass was used in the 1860s by prospectors headed into the Mosquito Mountain Range to find silver and gold. The Methodist Minister Father John Dyer mentions the pass in his 1860s autobiography *The Snowshoe Itinerant.*

Dr. John Evans was appointed by President Abraham Lincoln to be the Territorial Governor of Colorado. He was later asked to build a railroad across the Rocky Mountains, which he named the Denver, South Park and Pacific. The word "Denver" indicates the starting location of the railroad; the word "Pacific" its goal. Headed south from Como the rails passed Charles Hall's defunct salt works, and were spiked down across Trout Creek Pass in January of 1880. Two months later, rails were laid to Buena Vista on the Arkansas River.

47
MOSQUITO PASS

GPS Location: N 39° 16' 53" W 106° 11' 10"
Elevation: 13,186 feet
First road over top: 1878
County: Lake/Park
On BLM land
Pass requires high clearance four wheel drive vehicle

Father John L. Dyer tells the story of the naming of Mosquito Pass in his autobiography. In the spring of 1861, miners at a camp high on the east side of the Continental

North London Mine

Divide were trying to choose a name for their camp. Several names were suggested, none could be agreed upon, and the secretary recorded this in his book. When they met again, they found a smashed mosquito on the page of names, so they named the camp and the pass Mosquito.

John Dyer was born into a Methodist family in Madison County of Ohio on March 16, 1812. His parents taught him good work habits and Methodism. In 1832 he was licensed as an "exhorter" for the church. In 1851, he was ordained as a pastor. In 1833

The Mosquito Pass road.

CONTINENTAL DIVIDE—CENTRAL COLORADO

he married Harriet Foster, and they were blessed with five children. Harriet died in 1847. Dyer remarried quickly but then discovered that his new wife was not divorced from her first husband. He obtained a divorce from her and never remarried.

He chose to move to the Rocky Mountains to see Pike's Peak. After stopping in Denver to see his son Elias, he built his cabin in the Mosquito Mining Camp. In 1863 Colorado Methodists organized the "Rocky Mountain Conference" and appointed Dyer as a circuit riding pastor for today's Park, Lake, and Chaffee Counties.

To supplement his meager income, he took a mail route that required travel from the town of Buckskin Joe over Mosquito Pass to Oro City and California Gulch. The contract for the thirty-seven mile route required three trips per week. In the summer and early fall he rode a horse and during the winter he crossed the route on snowshoes. His snowshoes were the "Norway" style, skis that were from nine to eleven feet in length. He carried a long pole to remove sticking snow from the skis and to help with the up hill climbing and downhill braking. The route followed an old Indian trail over the Divide and was often times covered with fifteen to twenty feet of snow in the winter. He traveled at night, from 2 a.m. to 9 a.m., when the snow crust would support his weight.

John Dyer chose the following words for the title of his autobiography:

The
Snow-Shoe Itinerant
An Autobiography
Of the Rev. John L. Dyer
Familiarly known as "Father Dyer"

From the summit, the Mosquito Pass road heads down into Leadville.

CONTINENTAL DIVIDE—CENTRAL COLORADO

He used the word "itinerant" to describe his ministry. The dictionary defines the word as traveling from place to place. He used the word "familiar" to explain his usual title. Since the mining camps were filled with young men, the old preacher was respectfully called "Father."

In 1874, the first mine was opened east of Mosquito Pass on the north side of London Mountain. The problem of moving ore from the mine to the mill was solved by building an elevated rope cable-way, the first tramway built in Colorado. A second mine was opened on the south side of London Mountain in the 1890s. The two mines were connected by a tunnel through London Mountain, another first for Colorado mining.

A wagon road crossed Mosquito Pass in the early 1870s. When the Hayden Survey team mapped this area, they recorded that the pass and the road were named, but it was rough and designed mainly for walkers and mules. Construction of an improved wagon road was started in Leadville in November of 1878 and on the Fairplay side of the Divide in December of 1878. The Mosquito Pass Toll Road was completed in 1879. Mosquito Pass was the main route from Denver to Leadville until the railroads arrived in the Arkansas River Valley. Mosquito Pass is the highest pass for wheeled vehicles in the Rocky Mountains of Colorado.

48
WESTON PASS

GPS Location: N 39° 07' 53" W 106° 10' 56"
Elevation: 11,921 feet
First road over top: 1860
County: Lake/Park
Pike/San Isabel National Forest
Pass requires high clearance four wheel drive vehicle

The route over Weston Pass is an old Indian trail from South Park over the Mosquito Mountain Range into the Arkansas River Valley. In 1860, a wagon toll road was built on top of the Indian trail for the prospectors and miners headed for California Gulch near today's Leadville.

The pass is named for the Weston Brothers, Algernon and Philo. Philo arrived in Colorado in 1859 and settled on a 480-acre ranch. In 1862, he and his wife built and operated a roadhouse with a restaurant and sleeping rooms. He sold his property to Nathaniel Rich, his toll road gate keeper, and moved to Chaffee County. Algernon Weston arrived from Kansas in 1860 and bought a cattle ranch on the Leadville side of the pass. He sold his beef to store owners in the Leadville Mining District.

The town of Weston sprung up as a supply town on the South Park side of the Pass. In the late 1870s three freight companies were using the pass road, along with daily stagecoaches. At its peak, it was the busiest pass in Colorado, popular because it was protected from winter blizzards by Ptarmigan Peak on the north side of the pass road and by the Buffalo Peaks on the south side.

CONTINENTAL DIVIDE—CENTRAL COLORADO

The Weston Pass road climbs the east side of the pass to the summit.

49
TROUT CREEK PASS

GPS Location: N 36° 54' 36" W 105° 58' 30"
Elevation: 9,487 feet
First road over top: 1879
County: Chaffee/Park
San Isabel National Forest and public access through private land

The antelope and the buffalo were the first to use the salt springs that flow north and east of today's Antero Junction in South Park. The salt springs were later used by the Ute Indians and early settlers. Charles Hall homesteaded the springs in 1862 and started processing salt. In 1864, he incorporated the "Colorado Salt Works." John Q. A. Rollins, the founder of Rollinsville in Boulder County and builder of the Rollins Pass Road, was one of Hall's investors. By using a fireplace with a tall chimney, the salt brine was boiled and then placed into evaporation pans to air dry into salt crystals. Some of the salt was shipped to Denver for table use and some went to mining smelters to help remove minerals from the ore.

The U.S.G.S. Board on Geographic Names officially named the pass in 1906 for the creek starting near the top. This old Indian crossing was used in moving from South

CONTINENTAL DIVIDE—CENTRAL COLORADO

Imagine a bridge being supported by the two berms in this photograph. Now imagine that a Colorado Midland locomotive is crossing it at the same time that a Denver & South Park train is coming under the bridge directly at you. It must have been quite a sight.

Park into the Arkansas Valley. Going upstream on the South Platte River in South Park, Zebulon Pike's party crossed Trout Creek in 1806. This pass was heavily used by fur trappers and traders and later by prospectors and miners.

Two railroads crossed the pass, the narrow gauge Denver and South Park in January of 1880 and the standard gauge Colorado Midland in the summer of 1887. The South Park Railroad discontinued train service over Trout Creek in 1910, while the Colorado Midland operated until 1921. The sloped berms remain which were built to support a bridge creating an over-pass at Trout Creek Pass for the Colorado Midland to cross the rails of the South Park Railroad.

50
CURRANT CREEK PASS

GPS Location: N 38° 50' 13" W 105° 38' 10"
Elevation: 9,470 feet
First road over top: 1860
County: Park
On BLM Land

Cañon City, Colorado originated as a railroad station created by the Denver and Rio Grande Railroad in July of 1874. Citizens of Cañon City used a Ute Indian trail to build a road north to the mining town of Tarryall located west of today's town of Fairplay.

CONTINENTAL DIVIDE—CENTRAL COLORADO

Cañon City's good wagon road was built in 1860. A map produced by the Hayden Surveyors in 1875 named this pass the "Thirty Nine Pass" because it is located thirty-nine miles north of Cañon City.

We do not know who named the pass Currant Creek, but it was probably because of the growth of small seedless raisins along the creek coming off of the pass. The full name for currant is "Raison De Coravante," Raisins of Corinth, in Greek.

A town site was located at the junction of Smith Gulch and Currant Creek in 1868, a post office was opened in 1870, and a school opened in 1871. Ranching was the main industry supported by the town of Currant Creek. When the high country mining activity increased on the west side of South Park, this road was used to supply beef on the hoof to the mining camps on the Mosquito Range. When the post office was closed in 1901, the nearby town of Guffey became the area's business center.

Zebulon Pike recorded having crossed this low pass in 1806 and Captain John Fremont did so in 1844. Some pictographs have been found on rock overhangs near the pass. The Colorado Highway Department used this wagon road route for today's paved automobile road named State Highway 9.

51
LA SALLE PASS

GPS Location: N 39° 05' 06" W 105° 32' 43"
Elevation: 9,733 feet
First road over top: 1860s
County: Park
Pike National Forest

This pass is named for Samuel La Salle, a prospector who chose to make his home next to Tarryall Creek in the southeast corner of South Park. He built his wagon road over this low divide with the help of his neighbors. This new road became a well-used westerly crossing through the Puma Hills into South Park.

La Salle Pass is on the divide between Martland and Badger Peaks. The pass is three miles due north of Wilkerson Pass. It was used as the main road from the town of Mountaindale, now called Tarryall, west to the town of Hartsel and Trout Creek Pass and down into the Arkansas River Valley.

CONTINENTAL DIVIDE—CENTRAL COLORADO

52
WILKERSON PASS

GPS Location: N 39° 02' 17" W 105° 31' 32"
Elevation: 9,502 feet
First road over top: 1880
County: Park
Pike National Forest

The earliest use of this crossing was by Indians going across South Park to the hot springs near today's town of Colorado Springs. They came to visit their "Great Manitou," a supernatural force that according to one Indian tribe pervades the natural world. Indians all over Colorado used hot springs mineral water for physical and spiritual healing. The tribe that used this pass the most were the Ute Indians. Ute Pass is on the ridge crossing at the town of Divide west of Colorado Springs.

In July of 1875, Franklin Rhoda led the San Juan Division of the United States Government's Hayden Surveyors over the low pass now called Wilkerson. John Wilkerson came from Missouri after the Civil War to visit a friend and stayed to farm and ranch. While he was here, he named the pass after his family.

By 1880 a stage line from Colorado Springs crossed this pass on its way to Leadville. The stage station on the pass was called "The Illinois House" and was still in use in 1898. The stage route headed west across South Park through today's town of Hartsel to Trout Creek Pass. The route followed Trout Creek down to the Arkansas River Valley and today's Buena Vista. The stage route continued north through Granite into Leadville.

In the 1880s, James Hagerman built his standard gauge Colorado Midland Railroad through Eleven Mile Canyon into South Park. In 1921, the railroad failed, the railroad bed was abandoned, and highway traffic used the road bed. When the Eleven Mile Canyon Reservoir and State Park was built in Eleven Mile Canyon in 1931, U.S. Highway 24 was moved north to Wilkerson Pass.

SAN JUAN COUNTRY

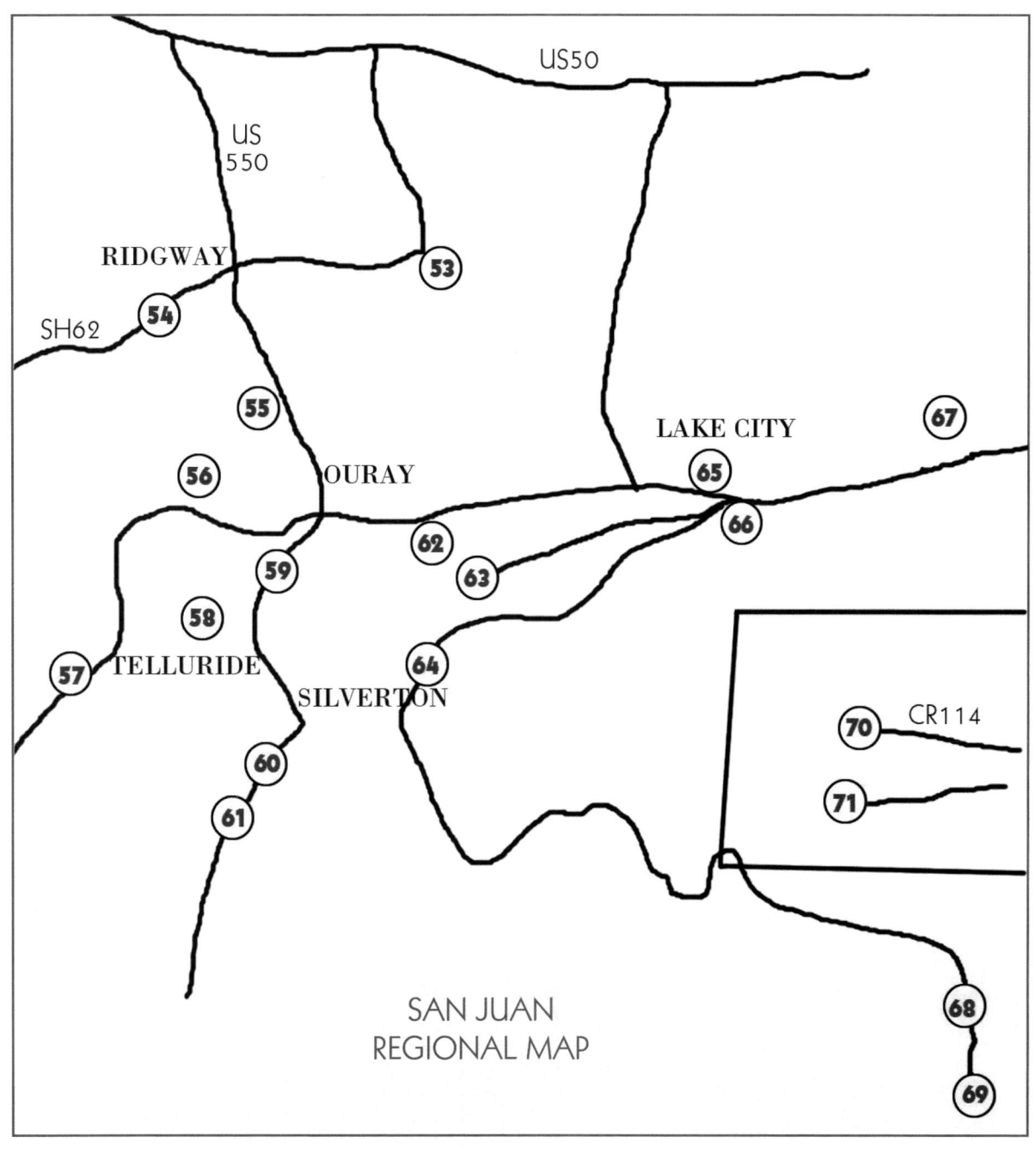

SAN JUAN REGIONAL MAP

53 Owl Creek Pass	59 Red Mountain Pass	66 Spring Creek Pass
Town of Ouray	60 Molas Pass	Town of Lake City
54 Dallas Divide	61 Coal Bank Pass	67 Los Pinos Pass
55 Black Bear Pass	62 Engineer Pass	68 Wolf Creek Pass
Town of Telluride	63 Cinnamon Pass	69 Elwood Pass
56 Imogene Pass	Town of Silverton	70 North Cochetopa Pass
57 Lizard Head Pass	64 Stony Pass	
58 Ophir Pass	65 Slumgullion Pass	71 Cochetopa Pass

SAN JUAN COUNTRY

53
OWL CREEK PASS

GPS Location: N 39° 09' 30" W 107° 33'44"
Elevation: 10,114 feet
First road over top: early 1960s
County: Gunnison/Ouray
Uncompahgre National Forest

The Owl Creek Road runs east from U.S. 550 north of Ridgway to cross Owl Creek Pass on the Cimarron Ridge mountains in the Uncompahgre National Forest. After crossing the pass, the road goes north through the Cimarron River Valley to U.S. 50 and the Gunnison River. A U.S. Forest Service map dated 1923 shows a road from north of Ridgway to Owl Creek Pass. The Court House Mountain Topo map of 1963 shows a road from the town of Cimarron to Owl Creek Pass. The early 1960s could be the date for the first road over the pass.

The Cimarron Ridge was formed by volcanic eruptions millions of years ago. As the soft rock was eroded and blown away, only the hard rock of the core remained standing. The result looks like a horizontal spine carved by a sculptor. Some of the

In John Wayne's movie "True Grit," this meadow was the setting for the final gunfight with Chimney Peak in the background.

rocks on the ridge south of Owl Creek Pass are named Chimney Peak and Courthouse Mountain. The rocks north of the pass are named Castle Rock, the Sawtooth Rocks, and the Washboard Rocks.

The "Bostwick Park" area was settled in the early 1880s. The park is located on the south side of the Gunnison River from the Cimarron River west to the area of Cerro Summit. The settlers were farmers and sheep or cattle ranchers, growing their own grass hay, alfalfa, and small grains for feed. In the early 1900s, irrigation water was supplied by private canal and reservoir companies. In the 1950s the U.S. Bureau of Reclamation conducted feasibility studies for building a major reservoir on the headwaters of the Cimarron River. On September 2, 1964, the U.S. Congress approved construction of the Silver Jack Reservoir about twenty-four miles south of the Gunnison River. Construction of the "Bostwick Park Project" started on October 21, 1966, and the first water was released in June of 1972. The reservoir water was released into the north flowing Cimarron River for use by the ranchers and farmers of Bostwick Park and the Cimarron Valley. This reservoir still participates in the "Colorado River Storage Project."

The Silver Jack Reservoir is about fifteen miles, as the eagle flies, from the Silver Jack Mine on Silver Mountain. Was the name "Silver Jack" used for the mine and reservoir? Or, did it belong to a man or to an animal?

A western movie was filmed in and around Ridgway in 1969. The leading actors for the movie "True Grit" were Ms. Kim Darby, Robert Duvall, Glen Campbell and the "Duke," John Wayne. The final "Shoot-out" between John Wayne and the bad guys was filmed in the Meadow just below Owl Creek Pass with Chimney Peak in the background.

TOWN OF OURAY

It is recorded that two prospectors from Silverton were the first white men to enter the Ouray Amphitheater. John Eckles and A. W. Begole came to Ouray over Engineer Pass and down the Uncompahgre River in 1875. Friends followed them into Ouray, which they named "Uncompahgre City." The translation of the Ute Indian word "uncompahgre" is "red water springs."

When the post office opened in 1875 the town was named for Ouray, the popular leader of the Tabeguache "band" of Ute Indians. The incorporation of the town followed with the first election in April of 1877. By 1878 the Bank of Ouray was opened, telephone service was installed to Silverton, Lake City and Mineral Point, and the Presbyterians had built Ouray's first church.

In June of 1883, Otto Mears started building a toll road south out of Ouray up high on the side of the Uncompahgre Canyon and Red Mountain Creek by dynamiting out a shelf road. The road was mostly a one lane road with occasional passing spots. He built his toll gate at Bear Creek Falls. He constructed this twelve mile road to the summit of Red Mountain Pass, completing it on November, 21, 1883.

In 1887 the Denver and Rio Grande Railroad graded a road bed and laid rails from the town of Montrose south through what would become the town of Ridgway and into the town of Ouray. This made possible cheaper passenger and freight costs into Ouray.

SAN JUAN COUNTRY

One pass road that starts in Ouray and goes southwest is called Imogene. It served the Sneffels Mines and Tom Walsh's Upper and Lower Camp Bird Mines. The other pass road south out of Ouray is called Red Mountain. The Black Bear Pass road begins at the Red Mountain Pass summit.

54
DALLAS DIVIDE

GPS Location: N 38° 05' 40" W 107° 53' 18"
Elevation: 8,970 feet
First road over top: 1882
County: Ouray/San Miguel
Public access through private land

The small townsite of Dallas was located two and one-half miles north of today's town named Ridgway. The divide named Dallas is nine miles west of Ridgway. The town and the divide honor George M. Dallas, vice-president of the United States from 1845 to 1849.

The first recorded crossing of this low divide was by two Roman Catholic priests named De Escalante and Dominguez. They were sent from Santa Fe, New Mexico, to

To maintain grading, the Rio Grande Southern Railroad crews built trestles across gullies and gulches.

SAN JUAN COUNTRY

Mount Sneffels (14,150') can be seen when descending Dallas Divide into Ridgway.

find a route that would connect the Spanish New Mexico missions with the California missions. They crossed this pass in 1776.

In 1882, Otto Mears chartered and built a toll road from Dallas over this divide to Telluride. In 1889 and 1890, Mears' Rio Grande Southern Railroad laid tracks over this divide. A train station was built and a post office opened at the small town at the top of the pass. The railroad was abandoned and the rails removed in the 1950s.

55
BLACK BEAR PASS

GPS Location: N 37° 53' 48" W 107° 42' 50"
Elevation: 12,840 feet
First road over top: 1800s
County: San Juan/San Miguel
San Juan/Uncompahgre National Forest
Pass requires high clearance, short wheel base, four wheel drive vehicle

The Black Bear road was built from the top of Red Mountain Pass to reach the Black Bear Mine on the side of Telluride Peak. The Black Bear road crosses the pass at the elevation of 12,840 feet, two and one half miles west of "The Million Dollar Highway."

SAN JUAN COUNTRY

The infamous switchbacks of Black Bear Pass as seen from Imogene Pass. Photo credit: Joe Eaglesfether

The road continues into Telluride past mines on the side of Ajax Peak in Ingram Basin and down into Telluride.

Tellurium is a rare metallic element related to sulphur, usually combined with gold and/or silver, discovered by prospectors in mines along the Black Bear Road. The town below the switchbacks and Bridal Veil Falls was named "Telluride." The miners who used the switchbacks on the face of Ingram Peak called them the "To Hell You Ride" road.

The longest free-falling waterfall in Colorado is Bridal Veil Creek's waterfall into the box canyon below. The altitude at the top of the falls is 10,279 feet. A hydro-electric plant was built at the top of the falls in 1895 to produce alternate current electricity for the Smuggler-Union and Tomboy Mines above Telluride. It was the third alternate current generating plant built in the United States. The first generating plant was built at Ames, southwest of Telluride. It was designed and built by Lucien L. Nunn, with the help of George Westinghouse and Nikola Tesla's inventions. See Lizard Head Pass (pg. 119) for more details of Nunn's electricity plants. The second electric plant was built at Ilium to provide a back-up for Nunn's Ames Plant and to increase the capacity of his system. He built high voltage lines to connect the two plants. Ilium is located five miles north of Ames.

TOWN OF TELLURIDE

John Fallon, M.R. White, J.F. Gundaker, John Summa, J.B. Ingram, and Charles Savage were the first prospectors to stake placer and lode claims in the upper San Miguel River Valley. At first they called their townsite "Columbia." The new name of Telluride was chosen because ore containing the element "tellurium" was discovered in the mines above their town.

In 1880, Otto Mears chartered and built a toll road in the San Juans starting north of Ridgway. The road was built west over Dallas Divide to Placerville, then upstream along the San Miguel River to Vance Junction. In November of 1889, Otto Mears sent his locating engineer, Charles W. Gibbs, to survey a route for a railway from Dallas Junction to Telluride. Otto Mear's railroad was called the Rio Grande Southern. The rail layers completed construction into Telluride on November 23, 1890. In July of 1891, rails were laid two and one-half miles to Pandora for the use of the Smuggler-Union Mine and Mill above Telluride. Telluride was an important supply center with all of the usual stores, stables, and saloons by 1878. Among the mines served were the famous Tomboy and Smuggler Mines. The Rio Grande Southern continued building their rails south over the Ophir Loop and Lizard Head Pass to Rico, down the Dolores River, and into Durango. The distance between Ridgway and Durango, the route of the Rio Grande Southern, is 162 miles.

On June 24, 1889, Roy Parker, Tom McCarty, and Matt Warner robbed the San Miguel Valley Bank in Telluride of about $21,000. Parker had stashed fresh horses outside of town and easily outran a chasing posse. Parker moved to Rock Springs, Wyoming and started working in a butcher shop using the name of George Cassidy. He was nicknamed "Butch" and because of his first successful robbery he went on to rob many more banks.

There are two pass roads that enter Telluride. The Black Bear Road starts at the top of Red Mountain Pass headed west over Black Bear Pass. It continues through Ingram Basin and down the notorious switchbacks into Telluride. The Imogene Pass Road starts in Ouray headed southwest up through the Camp Bird Mines to the top of the pass. The road runs down past the Tomboy and Smuggler-Union Mines into Telluride.

SAN JUAN COUNTRY

56
IMOGENE PASS

GPS Location: N 37° 55' 55" W 107° 44' 10"
Elevation: 13,114 feet
First road over top: 1960s
County: Ouray/San Miguel
Uncompahgre National Forest
Pass requires high clearance four wheel drive vehicle

Today's Imogene Pass Road begins on the south side of Ouray using the Camp Bird road built by Otto Mears in 1883 as a toll road. The pass road and pass were named for Andy Richardson's wife. Richardson worked with Tom Walsh as a mining engineer for the Camp Bird Mines. The "Camp Bird" name is borrowed from the Gray Jay, who is nick-named the "The Camp Robber."

Tom Walsh had been prospecting in the Leadville Mining District at the end of their silver boom. His best discovery in Leadville was his school teacher wife Carrie. The silver crash of 1893 wiped out almost everything they had earned. Tom, Carrie, and their two children moved to Ouray. While working up in today's Imogene Basin, Walsh found a lot of abandoned mines. He was able to buy up claims for very little money. In one of his new claims he discovered gold in tellurium form in a three-foot-wide vein of quartz.

The Camp Bird Mine began operations in 1896 in the upper Imogene Basin. In 1898, a mill was completed at the junction of Sneffels and Imogene Creeks. The Hidden Treasure Mine had been opened in 1875. Walsh bought it in 1896 and it was one of his biggest producers. By 1900 the Camp Bird properties included over 100 mining claims producing three to four million dollars annually. The Camp Bird Mine with its six-mile vein of gold became one of the largest gold mines in the world at that time.

In 1900 the Telluride Power Transmission Company built an AC electric line over Imogene Pass to bring power to the Camp Bird mines. Tom Walsh's miners were provided with housing that included real beds with mattresses and porcelain tubs. His three story boarding house was steam heated and equipped with electric lights. His mine tunnels had electric lights. The mine locomotives were also powered by electricity and he provided air compressor drills for removing the ore in the tunnels. In 1902 Walsh sold the Camp Bird Mines to a London Syndicate for $5.2 million dollars. Walsh then moved his family to Washington, D.C. Over the following years the mine changed hands many times.

On the way down the pass road into Telluride, the Smuggler and Tomboy mines experienced violent strikes by the Western Federation of Miners Union in 1901. In order to escape with their lives, the strike-breakers tried to cross Imogene Pass. The governor sent the Colorado State Militia to keep the trouble makers from entering the Camp Bird Mines. The ruins of several small buildings on the pass were called "Fort Peabody" and provided housing and protection for the militia.

SAN JUAN COUNTRY

57
LIZARD HEAD PASS

GPS Location: N 37° 48' 40" W 107° 54' 22"
Elevation: 10,322 feet
First road over the top: mid-1870s
County: Dolores/San Miguel
San Juan/Uncompahgre National Forest

This pass takes its name from Lizard Head Peak two and one-half miles northwest of the Pass. This peak has an unusual rock formation that has been described as a lizard head looking out of the mountain. Right, it doesn't look like that to me either! Today's highway 145 crosses the pass between Rico on the south and Ames on the north.

The route was first used by the early Spanish explorers, and more recently by prospectors, fur trappers, and traders. This trail was first used in the mid-1830s. A wagon road was built over Lizard Head Pass in the mid-1870s.

In 1890-91 Otto Mears built his longest railroad, The Rio Grande Southern, from Ridgway to Durango. The rails continued to Ophir, where in six months' time the Ophir Loop was built to gain elevation necessary to build across Lizard Head Pass. The railroad reached Durango in December of 1891.

Lucien L. Nunn arrived in Leadville in 1880 from Boston where he had studied law. He moved into Telluride, finished his law studies, and was admitted to the bar. He

The first hydro-electric plant to produce alternating current electricity was built at Ames.

began buying up mining claims including the Gold King Mine, three miles above the Ophir Loop, while working in banking in Telluride.

Wood was used as fuel for operating mining equipment and was quickly becoming scarce. In May of 1890 Nunn wrote his brother Paul urging him to meet and work with George Westinghouse to begin producing alternate current electricity.

L. L. and Paul Nunn worked with Westinghouse to build a hydroelectric plant at Ames located on the South Fork of the San Miguel River at the north end of the Lizard Head Pass Road. Earlier Lucien had bought water rights on the San Miguel River to run a stamp mill. Westinghouse brought a generator and motor to the project. He also brought Nikola Tesla's inventions, an alternate current induction motor called the Tesla Coil, and a method for the transmission of electricity through wires. Westinghouse hired Tesla to work for him on this and other ideas about alternate current electricity.

Water diverted from the San Miguel River dropped in a waterfall to spin a waterwheel connected by a belt to the generator. The generator drove a six-foot copper wired pelton wheel. The 75 kilowatt Westinghouse Alternator generated electricity at three thousand volts, 133 hertz single phase alternate current.

The first electricity was transmitted two and one-half miles to run a stamp mill at Nunn's Gold King Mine. The transmission line used was Western Union Cross Arms with insulators carrying two bare copper wires.

The Nunns and other investors formed the Telluride Power Company. The Ames Hydroelectric Plant was the first plant to produce and transmit alternate current electricity in the world. In 1891 they transmitted electricity to the Smuggler-Union, Liberty Bell, and Tomboy Mines above Ouray and Telluride. Using a transmission line over Imogene Pass, Nunn also provided electricity for the town of Ouray. In 1907 the Smuggler-Union Mine built their own hydroelectric plant using Bridal Veil Falls above Telluride. Nunn built his second plant in 1900 at Ilium, five miles down stream from the Ames plant as a back up for Ames and to increase his capacity to produce electricity.

Today's Ames Power Station was built in 1905, and uses two pelton wheels to produce 2400 volts and 1082 amperes for Excel Energy.

58

OPHIR PASS

GPS Location: N 37° 51' 02" W 107° 46' 46"
Elevation: 11,789 feet
First road over top: 1881
County: San Juan/San Miguel
San Juan/Uncompahgre National Forest
Pass requires high clearance four wheel drive vehicle

In the Bible's book of First Kings, Chapter Nine, Verses 26-28 we are told that King Solomon "Built a fleet of ships on the shore of the Red Sea" and that they were sent "to Ophir and brought from there gold." The gold was to be used "in the new King's house

This is a view of the long shelf road from the town of Ophir to the summit. An early spring snow makes the pass road visible.

and Temple." The person who named the town of Ophir and the mountain pass must have been a gold miner who knew the Old Testament of the Bible. There are as many ideas about the location of the Ophir Gold Mines as there are about Atlantis, the island in the Atlantic Ocean that legend says sank to the bottom of the ocean.

Some early maps of the Ophir area call this 11,789 foot pass "Howard Pass" named for Lt. George Howard, an early prospector in the area. A toll road was built from the Red Mountain Pass road starting at "Burro Bridge" by James Mountain in 1881. The road followed an old Indian trail to the top of the pass, and then descended on the longest shelf road in the San Juan Mountains to the town of Ophir. The town was located in the Howard Fork Valley of the San Miguel River at the base of the pass. The town's often moved post office is now next to today's Highway 145. James Mountain called his road The Silverton and Ophir Toll Road.

Otto Mears incorporated his Rio Grande Southern Railroad on November 5, 1889. His railway would start at Dallas Junction, later named Ridgway to honor the first superintendent of the R.G.S. The railroad's terminus was the town of Durango.

On June 20, 1890, the first rails at Dallas Junction were in place. The 490-acre townsite of Ridgway was platted in June of 1890. A railroad station with housing, shop, roundhouse, and rail yard was also constructed. The rails were laid west over Dallas Divide to Placerville. They continued up the San Miguel River and arrived at Vance Junction on November 16, 1890. Heading south, the rails of the Rio Grande Southern were built on the west side of San Miguel River Canyon until they crossed over the high "Butterfly Bridge" which crosses the Howard Fork of the San Miguel River. This Butterfly Bridge was named not because of its shape or design, but rather because it crossed below the Butterfly Mine. After crossing the river, the rails were built on trestles and shelf roads on the side of Yellow Mountain to a twenty-four degree hair

SAN JUAN COUNTRY

Looking down from the pass, we see the beginning of the long shelf road to Ophir.

pin curve using a 3¼ percent grade rise called the "Ophir Loop." After the loop, the "High Line" rails were headed west over trestles to the Lake Fork of the San Miguel River and climbed south around Trout Lake to cross Lizard Head Pass. It is interesting to note that because of the topography, about 80 percent of the High Line section was built on trestles. The R.G.S. built southwest to Rico, then southeast to Dolores and Mancos, and then east to end in Durango.

Because of the Rio Grande Southern Railroad on the west end of Ophir Pass and the Silverton Railroad, on the east end, the Ophir Road was no longer needed or used. The current road was opened in 1953 for back country enthusiasts.

SAN JUAN COUNTRY

59
RED MOUNTAIN PASS

GPS Location: N 37° 53' 56" W 107° 42' 43"
Elevation: 11,018 feet
First road over top: November 1884
County: Ouray/San Juan
San Juan/Uncompahgre National Forest

The history of Red Mountain Pass must begin with the words "red mountains." There are three Red Mountains in a one square mile area on the east side of today's Highway 550. It is the oxidized iron content in the rocks that gives the red-orange color to these mountains.

United States surveyors were the first people exploring in these mountains. In the summer of 1874, Franklin Rhoda's team of the Hayden Survey Party climbed these mountains to set elevations and to map them. In 1875 William Marshall led the Wheeler survey team through the San Juans.

The Yankee Girl mine was considered the mother lode in the Red Mountain Mining District. The Yankee Girl shaft house sat over a chimney of silver ore 1000' deep.

SAN JUAN COUNTRY

The names of the mines and the towns in the Red Mountain Mining District are given as background to the real story of Red Mountain Pass, the building of the twenty-six mile road over the mountains from Ouray to Silverton. The towns are Albany, Ironton, Guston, Red Mountain Town, Congress, and Chattanooga. Some of the best known silver mines are the Silver Ledge, Silver Crown, Carbon Lake, Hudson, Salem, Congress, Guston, Genessee, National Belle, and Yankee Girl. The Yankee Girl was the richest and most famous silver mine in the United States.

Ironton was the home of the Corkscrew Gulch railroad turntable. It was used to drop trains down from the main line into Ironton Park. It was the only known turntable covered with a tall conical roof for snow removal.

In March of 1883 Ouray County started a road headed south upstream along the Uncompahgre River. In June of 1883, Otto Mears was given a charter to complete that wagon road. His six-mile toll road to Ironton was opened in October of 1883.

San Juan County started building a road from Silverton to the Red Mountain Area which reached Chattanooga, the transfer point for freight hauled by mules hitched to wagons, then to mules forming a pack train carrying materials on their backs. In June of 1884, San Juan County gave Otto Mears a charter to build a wagon road from Silverton to the top of Red Mountain Pass. By November of 1884 he had completed the road to the Yankee Girl Mine. At that time Mears owned a six-mile road from Ouray to Ironton and a twelve-mile road from Silverton to Red Mountain Pass. In 1887-88 Mears brought his Silverton Railroad up to and over Red Mountain Pass. It enabled

This is a view of the Idarado Mine from across the valley on the original Red Mountain Pass road. Today's Red Mountain Pass road (Hwy 550) can be seen climbing up to the summit.

SAN JUAN COUNTRY

This photograph shows the townsite of Red Mountain Town. The original pass road can be seen going around the National Belle Mine to the summit.

the Red Mountain Mining District to move ore to mills and smelters in Silverton more cheaply than by wagons and mules.

Mears had a station on the pass called Sheridan Junction. His first train arrived at the "Junction" on September 17, 1888. When built the Silverton Railroad used the highest railroad pass in the United States. By 1921 this railroad route was no longer used, and it was officially abandoned in mid-1922. The charters, owned by Mears, had ended in 1900 and the counties acquired ownership of the entire road.

The Colorado Highway Commission was formed and funded in 1910 to build and maintain roads for automobiles. In July of 1922 a widening and upgrade was started from Ouray to Ironton. The road was closed to make it easier and faster to build. The road builders used the abandoned Silverton Railroad bed to continue the auto road on down to the Chattanooga Valley. A new road was built along the railroad bed into Silverton.

The last part of the upgrading from Ironton to Red Mountain Pass was completed in 1924. When the highway department met to accept the bid for construction someone said "we are building a million dollar highway" and the road has been called that ever since. The dedication of the new "Million Dollar Highway" was held on the pass on July 4, 1924. The extended part of the highway was completely paved with asphalt between 1953-1955.

SAN JUAN COUNTRY

West Needle Mountain Range from the summit of Molas Divide.

61 and 60
COAL BANK AND MOLAS DIVIDE

GPS Locations: Coal Bank: N 37° 42' 02" W 107° 46' 37"
Molas Divide: N 37° 44' 16" W 107° 41' 53"
Elevations: Coal Bank: 10,640 feet
Molas Divide: 10,910 feet
First road over top: 1877
County: San Juan
San Juan National Forest

The road headed north out of Durango was built to the San Juan Mountains following the Animas River Valley. When the road reached the entrance to the Animas Canyon it was moved west into the mountains. The road originally followed Lime Creek and later crossed Coal Bank Pass at the altitude of 10,640 feet. The black rocks looked like coal but were actually shale. In 1879, a forest fire burned 26,000 acres at what is now known as Lime Creek , almost to the town of Silverton. Seven miles north of Coal Bank Pass, the highway crosses Molas Pass at 10,910 feet and continues down to Silverton.

"Molas" is Spanish for "moles." Moles live in tunnels and burrow in the soft dirt around Molas Lake at the pass. The mole's body is tapered on both ends, enabling them to travel both frontwards and backwards. They have huge front feet and claws and very bad eyesight.

Both of these passes were on an ancient trail to enter the heart of the San Juan Mountains. Trappers, traders, and freighters spoke about the mining activity here in 1877. Baker's Park is the name given to the hourglass-shaped area with Silverton located on the south end and Animas Forks on the north end. When Baker would travel south out of the park, he could bypass the Animas River Canyon by crossing Molas and Coal Bank Passes. Molas and Coal Bank are about seven miles apart. A toll road was finished in 1882 from Silverton to Molas Lake.

A study in 1988 established that the cleanest and clearest views in the state are from Molas Pass. Monitors studied air pollution and visibility. The air at Molas Pass has the fewest number of particulates of anywhere in the state, allowing visibility of over 140 miles in any direction.

This photograph shows the Engineer Pass road going toward Animas Forks.

62
ENGINEER PASS

GPS Location: N 37° 58' 32" W 107° 35' 04.8"
Altitude: 12,806 feet
First road over top: 1877
County: Hinsdale/Ouray
On BLM land
Pass requires high clearance four wheel drive vehicle

The San Juan mining boom was under way when the wagon road over Engineer Mountain was built in August of 1877. It was the merchants of Lake City who built the Engineer Road to bring ore to their smelters. They named it the "Henson Creek and Uncompahgre Toll Road." It was built between Lake City and Mineral Point. Ouray, Silverton, and Lake City were busy mining camps hustling to become towns. Hundreds of miners were working in the mines and mills around Engineer Mountain in the camps called Capital City, Mineral Point, Animas Forks, and on American Flats.

    The Hayden survey team led by Ada D. Wilson and Franklin Rhoda headed west from Lake City in the summer of 1874 to reach the summit of Uncompahgre Peak. From the 14,309 foot peak they could measure and make maps of the San Juan Mountains. To get there they followed the prospector's trail up to the mining camp of Henson and then north to climb the peak. Uncompahgre Peak is eleven miles northeast of Engineer Mountain as the eagle flies.

The Red Mountain Pass road is today's U.S 550 headed south out of Ouray. Three and one-half miles up this road is a state-built bridge across the Uncompahgre River. The road to the left is the start of the Engineer Pass road. The first road to the right of this road runs to Poughkeepsie Gulch. The second road to the right leads to Mineral Point. The pass road continues switch-backing to a long shelf road that leads to the pass summit on the north side of Engineer Mountain. From the pass, the road crossed the American Flats mining district to head downstream along Henson Creek through Capital City, Henson, and into Lake City.

Here are some closing thoughts about Engineer Pass. It is written that in 1880 the "Rocky Mountain Stage and Express Service" ran stages from Lake City across Engineer Pass to Animas Forks. Rose's Cabin near the pass was a stage stop that provided a boarding house and stables. Several people have written that there was a short-cut road around the top of Engineer Mountain called Yvonne Pass. It was short-lived and abandoned. We do not have the name of the civil engineer who might have named this mountain and its rugged pass. We know for certain that the mining camp named Engineer City was started in 1874 as a tent camp in American Flats and that it was one of only two mining camps in the Colorado Rockies at the time without a saloon.

Henson Dam as it stands in the summer of 2012.

SAN JUAN COUNTRY

This picture of Cinnamon Mountain, on the right side, was taken from Burrows Park near the pass summit.

63
CINNAMON PASS

GPS Location: N 37° 56' 02" W 107° 32' 16"
Elevation: 12,620 feet
First road over top: 1877
County: Hinsdale/San Juan
On BLM Land
Pass requires high clearance four wheel drive vehicle

This pass is named for the mountain, which was named for the warm glow of the reddish tundra grasses growing from timberline to the summit of Cinnamon Mountain. Charles Baker was probably the first white man to cross this pass when he entered the San Juan Mountains in 1860. Albert Burrows explored and prospected this area in 1873, and a park is now named for him on the east side of the pass summit.

*This photograph shows the cinnamon colored rocks that gave this pass its name.
Photo Credit: Patt Jones*

SAN JUAN COUNTRY

Otto Mears chartered and started building a toll road in 1874 from Lake City up through the mining towns of Sherman and Argentum. After crossing the pass, the road entered the towns of Animas Forks, Eureka, and Howardsville and arrived in Silverton. His construction crews were supervised by his best friend and partner, Enos Hotchkiss.

The Hayden survey party working on the top of Uncompahgre Peak watched Mears' crews at work in the summer of 1874. Cairns used for triangulation by Hayden and Mears' men could possibly still be in place in the mountains. Mears' first road was only a slight upgrade from the early Indian trail and not passable by wagons. The only section of the Mears' road that wagons could use was from Animas Forks south. In 1877, Mears built a good wagon road from Lake City to Animas Forks.

TOWN OF SILVERTON

S. B. Kellog, H. A. W. Tabor's partner in Leadville's California Gulch, grubstaked Charles Baker to prospect for silver in the San Juan Mountains. Baker and his party went south out of Leadville in 1860 following the Arkansas River to Poncha Springs. They crossed the Continental Divide using Monarch Pass and followed Tomichi Creek to today's site of the town of Gunnison. They continued west to the site of today's town of Sapinero, and then went south along the Lake Fork of the Gunnison River to the area of today's Lake City. Heading west again they used what became the Cinnamon Pass road to enter the headwaters of the Animas River. They panned for silver and gold, naming the area "Baker's Park." Near Silverton, prospectors Reese, French, and Johnson discovered a large gold-bearing quartz vein in Arrasta Gulch.

In 1873, prospectors and miners chose a townsite at the confluence of Mineral and Cement Creeks with the Animas River. In 1874, the town of Silverton was platted on 320 acres and incorporated in 1876. The "Reese Hook and Ladder Company," the first volunteer firemen company in the San Juans, was started in 1876. The name of Silverton came from a miner who said "we ain't got much gold, but we've got silver by the ton."

The Denver and Rio Grande Railroad laid rails west out of Walsenberg over La Veta Pass and arrived in Alamosa in the summer of 1878. In 1880, the rails were spiked down south to Antonito. After crossing Cumbres Pass, the railroad arrived in Chama, New Mexico on February 1, 1881. The rails were built west to the new town of Durango, then north upstream above the Animas River to reach Silverton on July 3, 1882.

There were two mining areas north of Silverton that did not involve crossing a pass. Both were served by one of Otto Mears' railroads. The first was built northeast to Howardsville. From there, rails were laid north to Eureka and the large Sunnyside Mill. In 1903, the railroad entered the Animas Forks Mining District. The Silverton Northern Railroad was operational from 1893 to 1942. Silverton's second northern mining district was supported by Mears' Silverton, Gladstone and Northerly Railroad. Located six miles north of Silverton, the town of Gladstone was located on Cement Creek. Its largest mine was "The Gold King."

64
STONY PASS

GPS Location: N 37° 47' 43" W 107° 32' 58"
Elevation: 12,588 feet
First road over top: 1879
County: San Juan
Rio Grande National Forest/BLM land
On the divide
Pass requires high clearance four wheel drive vehicle

This old crossing was an early route from southeastern Colorado into the Animas River Valley of the San Juan Mountains. The first people to use this pass were the Ute Indians on their seasonal migrations. Some artifacts from Spain have been found near the top of the pass.

It is reported that Charles Baker discovered Stony Pass in 1860 looking for a road into the San Juans. This early route into the future location of the mining camps near Silverton and the Upper Animas River Valley started near today's town of Creede. The road went upstream along the Rio Grande River to Stony Pass on the Continental Divide. After crossing the Divide, the road went down to today's Howardsville and headed six miles south into today's Silverton. The initial reason for this road was to supply machinery and supplies to the Little Giant Mine three miles from Silverton. A wagon toll road was built over Stony by Major E. M. Hamilton in 1872 that he chartered as The Silverton and Grassy Hill Toll Road.

In August of 1874 Franklin Rhoda's team of the Hayden surveyors measured and mapped the 110 mile long Stony Pass Road from today's Creede to Silverton. In 1880 the Brewster Stage Company started carrying passengers and U.S. mail on this road into Silverton. After the Denver and Rio Grande Railroad reached Silverton in 1882, the Stony Pass Road was not used much.

In August of 1910 David Mechling and John McGuire drove the first automobile over Stony Pass. It was a thirty horsepower "Croxton-Keeton," made in Ohio, patterned after the French Renault. Because of the steepness of the road on both sides of the pass, the State Highway Department decided not to turn it into an automobile road.

Lake San Cristobal was formed when a large rockslide blocked today's lake fork of the Gunnison River.

65
SLUMGULLION PASS

GPS Location: N 37° 59' 08" W 107° 13' 20"
Elevation: 13,361 feet
First road over top: 1875
County: Hinsdale
Gunnison National Forest

In 1875, Franklin Rhoda, with his topographer Ada D. Wilson, led the San Juan Division of the Hayden Surveyors west along the Gunnison River to the Lake Fork of the Gunnison River and south to Lake City. When they arrived at Lake San Cristobal, near Lake City, they were so impressed with its beauty that they said that it was the finest lake they had seen in Colorado. The name "San Cristobal" is Spanish for "Saint Christopher." In their notes they also recorded the very large rock and mud slide of yellow material that had moved down to dam the river and create the lake.

During an extreme wet period about 850 years ago, a massive block of rock, dirt, and forest broke away from the face of "Mesa Seco." Slow moving land and mud slides altered an area 3,000 feet high and over four miles in length and changed the landscape of over 1,000 acres. The Slumgullion Earthflow blocked the Lake Fork of the Gunnison River and formed Lake San Cristobal. About 350 years ago another earthflow covered up about one-half of the original slide, and it is still active today, moving up to twenty feet per year.

The name Slumgullion was probably given to the slide for several reasons. The dictionary definition of the word slumgullion is "a meat stew with chunks of meat and roots." Because of its color it could have looked like that to the early prospectors. Another possibility is that the placer miners thought that the slide looked like the sediments left in their sluice boxes as they worked the streams and gullies for gold.

During the years of 1874 and 1875, Otto Mears built his "Saguache and San Juan Toll Road" starting from his hometown of Saguache on the western edge of the San Luis Valley. Mears' road crossed the Continental Divide at Cochetopa Pass and continued through the then towns of Cochetopa, Powderhorn, and Barnum. From Barnum the road went south into Lake City. His best friend and construction leader was Enos Hotchkiss, who while surveying for this toll road, discovered gold on the north side of Lake Cristobal. He called his mine "the Golden Fleece." A company town was formed to survey and sell Lake City lots in 1875. The post office was opened and Lake City eventually became the county seat. It was probably the fastest growing mining town in Colorado at that time. Someone estimated that close to 2,000 people lived in and around Lake City in the late 1870s.

Lake City got a railroad when The Denver and Rio Grande constructed a branch from its main line at the Gunnison River. It went south along the Lake Fork thirty-six miles to Lake City. It was opened for operation in August of 1889.

The headwall of Mesa Seco broke off and flowed down to create Lake San Cristobal.

SAN JUAN COUNTRY

66
SPRING CREEK PASS

GPS Location: N 37° 56' 27" W 107° 09' 33"
Elevation: 10,901 feet
First road over top: 1875
County: Hinsdale
Gunnison National Forest
On the Divide

On an army map drawn in 1851, R. H. Kern called this pass "The Pass of the Rio Del Norte." He was wrong because this was not the headwaters of the Rio Grande River, which the Spanish called Rio Del Norte. This pass was also called Cebola, Spanish for onion, for one of the creeks starting here on the west side of the Continental Divide.

We do not know who named the pass, but it is probably named for Big Spring Creek which starts on the Divide.

This low crossing is an old Ute Indian trail that they used to move out of the Gunnison River Valley into the eastern San Juans and the west side of the San Luis Valley. It was used by trappers, traders, and scouts headed north from Taos into the Arkansas and Gunnison River Valleys.

This is Clear Creek Falls where a stagecoach station was operated.

SAN JUAN COUNTRY

About six and one-half miles south of Spring Creek Pass, a stage station named Belford was operated by the Barlow and Sanderson Stage Company. From the station the passengers could see Clear Creek Falls and get meals and lodging. When the Denver and Rio Grande Railroad reached Gunnison in 1885 and later on built a spur into Lake City the Spring Creek road usage declined.

The citizens of today's town of Del Norte on the western edge of the San Luis Valley built a toll road west in order to increase their economy and compete with the town of Saguache. Their "Antelope Park Lake City Toll Road" was built from Del Norte to South Fork and then northwest to the small town of Wagon Wheel Gap. From Wagon Wheel Gap, the road followed the Rio Grande River into Antelope Park and then north over Spring Creek Pass and Slumgullion Pass into Lake City. Written history does not tell us if the Del Norte Toll Road was profitable for Del Norte's economy.

TOWN OF LAKE CITY

The Grand River Division of the Hayden Surveyors measured, mapped, and named the Lake City Area in 1875. They were there when Otto Mears and Enos Hotchkiss were building their Saguache and San Juan Toll Road into today's Lake City. Hotchkiss was a prospector and a surveyor/town builder. He discovered a rich vein of gold and silver and called his mine "The Golden Fleece." He also helped plat the townsite of Lake City.

Lake City was named because of the large Lake San Cristobal just south of town. From its beginning Lake City attracted settlers with families. Many ranchers, lumbermen, businessmen, and town developers chose to build homes and stores and made Lake City their permanent home. By 1877 four churches were built. The town created laws to protect its citizens and the lawmen enforced the town laws, which resulted in much less crime than occurred in most early mining towns.

The Engineer Pass road was built by the merchants of Lake City to reach today's town of Ouray. Starting at Lake City their road was built up-stream along Henson Creek to the mining camps of Henson and Capital City. After crossing today's Engineer Pass the road down Engineer Mountain followed the Uncompahgre River into today's town of Ouray. This road was built in the summers of 1877 and 1878. The first wagon road west out of Lake City was built in 1875 by Enos Hotchkiss and Otto Mears. It crossed Cinnamon Pass into the headwaters area of the Animas River. There has not been regular maintenance on the road since it was constructed.

Lake City residents wanted a railroad that would connect them with the town of Gunnison. Construction work was started at Sapinero by the Denver and Rio Grande Railroad in 1881. As always, the lack of money and short building seasons delayed this railway. The railroad was eventually completed from Gunnison west to Sapinero, then south along the Lake Fork of the Gunnison River to the town of Lake City.

The two passes that start and/or finish in Lake City are Engineer and Cinnamon. Two more passes coming from the southeast into Lake City are Spring Creek and Slumgullion. Nearby Spring Creek Pass crosses the Continental Divide; Slumgullion Pass does not.

SAN JUAN COUNTRY

67
LOS PIÑOS PASS

GPA Location: N 38° 06' 14" W 106° 28' 20"
Elevation: 10,420 feet
First road over top: mid 1870s
County: Saguache
Gunnison National Forest
Pass requires high clearance four wheel drive vehicle

In 1868, Nathaniel Taylor and Kit Carson escorted Chief Ouray and the leaders of the seven Ute Bands to Washington to sign the Ute Treaty of 1868. This treaty created two Indian agencies to support and protect the Utes. The Los Piños Agency was built on a tributary of Cochetopa Creek, later named Los Piños Creek. The White River Agency was built near today's town of Meeker. The agents were responsible for the distribution of the supplies and food promised by the treaty.

A second treaty was signed by Ouray and the Ute leaders with the U.S. Government in 1873. This treaty was called the Brunot Treaty, named for the U.S. Indian Commissioner Felix Brunot. Otto Mears served as the interpreter at this event. After two unqualified agents failed as leaders at Los Piños, General Charles Adams was placed in charge and he won the respect and trust of the Utes.

In August of 1874, the Hayden Survey team was measuring and mapping the Cochetopa Pass road. Their photographer William Jackson took several pictures of the Ute Indians and their lodges.

In 1875, the U.S. Government ordered the Ute Indians at the Los Piños Agency to be moved to the new Uncompahgre Agency. It was built near today's town of Colona on the Uncompahgre River. In 1875 and 1876, Otto Mears built the "Lake Fork and Ouray Toll Road" to allow wagons to bring supplies to the new agency. He started his toll road at Gateview. From there he built west through Cimmaron and over Cerro Summit into the future Montrose on the Uncompahgre River. He then built the road south to the new Ute Agency.

In 1879, Nathan Meeker tried to change the Indians at the White River Agency from being hunters and gatherers into farmers. His drastic efforts resulted in the Battle of Milk Creek and the Meeker Massacre. In 1880, the Northern Utes were forced out of Colorado to the Unitah Reservation in eastern Utah. The southern Utes were allowed stay on their reservations in southwest Colorado.

68
WOLF CREEK PASS

GPS Location: N 37° 28' 57" W 106° 47' 56"
Elevation: 10,850 feet
Road over top: 1916
County: Mineral
Rio Grande/San Juan National Forest
On the Continental Divide

This low crossing over the Continental Divide separates Wolf Creek on the west side and Pass Creek on the east side is called Wolf Creek Pass. Today's U.S. Highway 160 is the road over the pass. The creek and the pass were probably named for the early settler William Wolf.

In the 1820s, fur trappers and traders followed the Ute Indians who used the pass to go into the San Juan Mountains. The San Juan branch of Hayden's United States Geological and Geographical Survey measured and mapped the Wolf Creek area in 1873. The use of this route as a trail continued until the Colorado Highway Commission was created and funded in 1909. In 1913, construction was started on the first road to be built over Wolf Creek Pass. The road headed west out of Walsenburg to cross over La Veta Pass into the San Luis Valley and through today's towns of Alamosa, Monte Vista, and Del Norte. Then the road would cross Wolf Creek Pass on the Continental Divide at the elevation of 10,850 feet. The road continued through Pagosa Springs to Durango. Completed in 1916, this new road was the first automobile road over the Continental Divide.

69
ELWOOD PASS

GPS Location: N 37° 24' 23" W 106° 38' 40"
Elevation: 11,660 feet
First road Over Top: 1878
County: Rio Grande
Rio Grande/San Juan National Forest
On the divide
No road over the top today

Elwood Pass is located on the Continental Divide ten miles southeast of today's Wolf Creek Pass. The pass was named by and for the early settler T. L. Woodvale. He used the "L" from his middle name, put an "E" in front of it, and the first part of his last name to call it Elwood Pass.

SAN JUAN COUNTRY

These cabins are some of the buildings left standing in the town of Summitville.

The Ute Indians crossed this high pass to use the healing hot springs at today's Pagosa Springs. The Ute word "Pagosa" describes the sulphur odor of the Hot Springs' water.

In 1877, a charter was granted to the Conejos, Pagosa Springs and Rio Grande Toll Road Company to build a road over the Continental Divide using Elwood Pass. The road was built and the U.S. mail was carried from Summitville over the pass to Pagosa Springs. In 1878, the U.S. Army used soldiers to build a wagon road over Elwood Pass to move men and materials from Fort Garland in the San Luis Valley to Fort Lewis at Pagosa Springs. Until the construction of Wolf Creek Pass, Elwood was the most often used crossing from the San Juans to the San Luis Valley.

The town of Summitville was built two miles east of Elwood Pass and was the largest mining camp of the district. Gold, silver, copper, and other minerals were discovered on the divide's east side. Many well built cabins and store buildings were left standing when the mining and the town ended in 1889.

The road over Elwood Pass did go to Timberhill, the Elwood ghost town and Summitville until it was washed out by a gully washer rain in October of 1911.

SAN JUAN COUNTRY

70
NORTH COCHETOPA PASS

GPS Location: N 38° 13' 00" W 106° 34' 32"
Elevation: 10,149 feet
First road over top: 1872
County: Saguache
Gunnison/Rio Grande National Forest
On the Continental Divide

In his search for a railroad route through the Rocky Mountains, Captain John W. Gunnison mapped Cochetopa Pass in August of 1853. Its low elevation and wide open space made it a perfect place to cross with a railroad. However, rails were never laid on Cochetopa Pass. A wagon road had been built on this new northern route across the Continental Divide by 1872. This road was developed into a toll road by 1875.

Two miners prospecting in the Cochetopa Hills in 1880 discovered native gold southeast of Cochetopa Canyon. In October of 1880 the town site of Cochetopa was open for settlers, miners, and business people. By the end of November it boasted of grocery and hardware stores, saloons, and stables. By the summer of 1881 the town was incorporated with over twenty buildings including a post office. Another prospector discovered ancient Spanish mines in the vicinity of the townsite.

In 1882 the mines collapsed because the ore did not exist in money-making quantities. The North Pass over the Continental Divide is crossed by today's State Highway 114 from Saguache to Gunnison. The highway was upgraded and paved for an automobile road in 1962.

71
COCHETOPA PASS

GPS Location: N 38° 09' 59.9" W 107° 41' 53"
Elevation: 10,067 feet
First road over top: August, 1824
County: Saguache
Gunnison/Rio Grande National Forest
On the Continental Divide

Cochetopa is the English version of the Ute Indian word "Kuchupupan" meaning buffalo passing. This pass road is one of the ancient buffalo trails over the Continental Divide. It was also used by the Ute Indians to move from the Gunnison Country to winter in the San Luis Valley.

SAN JUAN COUNTRY

In August of 1824 Antoine Robidoux left Taos, New Mexico, with a group of fourteen people and traveled north through the San Luis Valley to the future site of the town of Saguache. From there he headed west into the Cochetopa Hills to cross the Continental Divide. Robidoux is reported as being the first person to lead wheeled vehicles across this pass, which also was the first crossing of the Continental Divide in Colorado. Robidoux was a fur trader and guide of French ancestry, who married a Mexican woman and became a Mexican citizen. From the pass he followed the headwaters of the Gunnison River west, arriving at its junction with the Uncompahgre River in the summer of 1828. He built his first trading post near present-day Delta. In the early 1830s he built a second trading post on the Yampa River which he called Fort Robidoux. From there his men hunted and set traps in the Trappers Lake and Flattop Mountains area.

There is a bronze plaque erected by the State Historical Society of Colorado on Old Cochetopa Pass in 1929 that marks the summit. The plaque has one error. It lists the elevation at 10,032 feet; it is now recognized to be 10,067 feet.

In 1853 the U.S. Congress approved the use of their topographical engineers to find a good railroad route east-to-west across the Colorado Rocky Mountains. They selected Captain John Gunnison to head up the expedition which was escorted by mounted riflemen, sixteen six-mule wagons to carry needed travel supplies, an instrument wagon, and an ambulance. They left Missouri on the Santa Fe Trail early in June of 1853. By August they were in Colorado at the Arkansas River and they camped near today's town of Saguache on August 29. After crossing the pass on September 2, they followed the Indian trail west along Tomichi Creek and the Gunnison River. They continued across Western Colorado and were exploring the Sevier River in Utah on October 26 when they were attacked by Paiute Indians. The Indians killed Captain Gunnison, his artist, botanist, and five others. Lt. Edward Beckwith took command of the expedition and led it to California. Cochetopa Pass would have been a good crossing for a railroad, but it has never been used for that purpose.

The Hayden Surveyors "Atlas of Colorado" shows two different pass roads over the Cochetopa Hills. The route that they identify as Cochetopa is actually "North Cochetopa Pass," four plus miles north of Cochetopa Pass and is the route now used for Colorado Highway Fourteen.

CONTINENTAL DIVIDE—SOUTHERN COLORADO

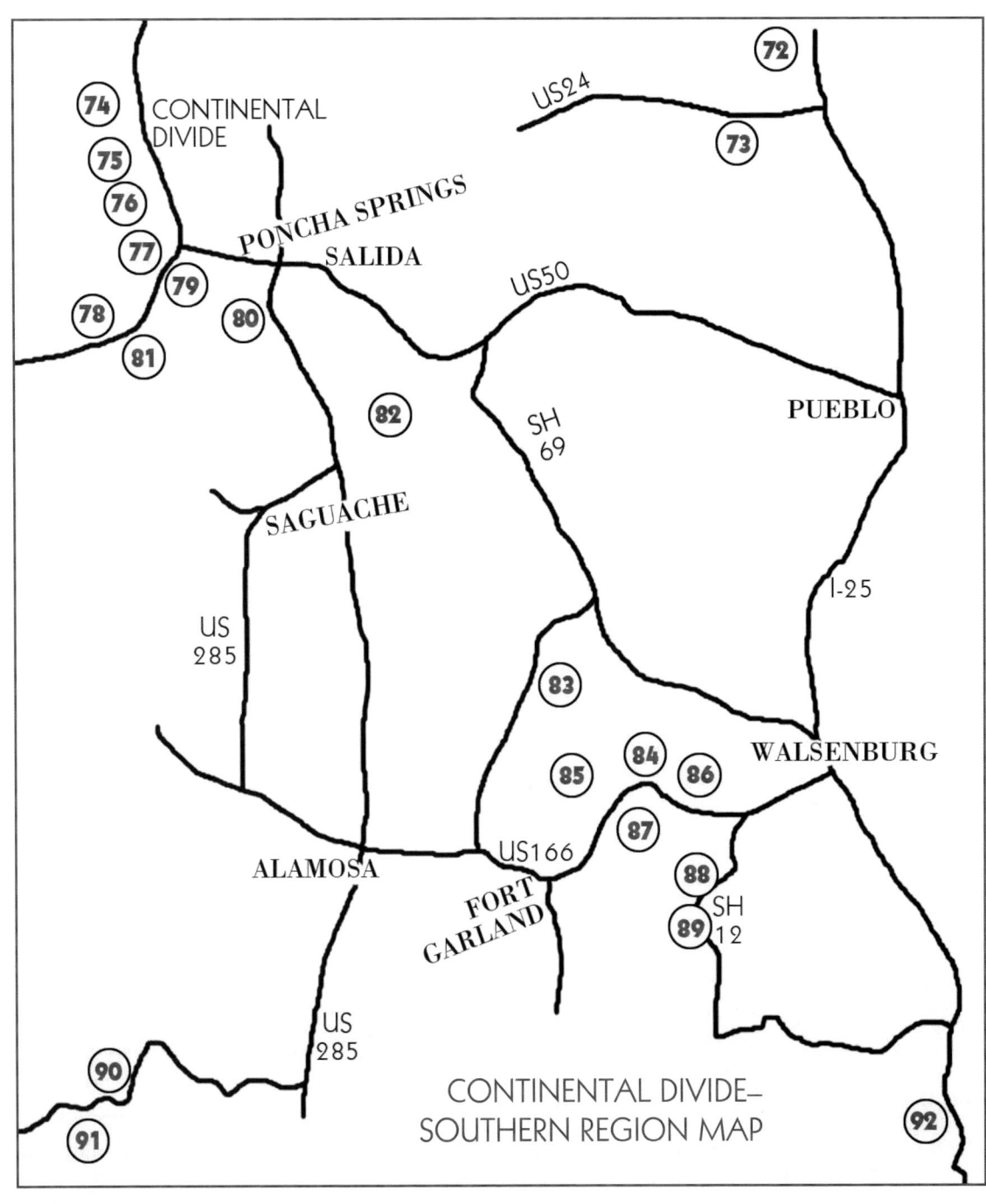

CONTINENTAL DIVIDE—
SOUTHERN REGION MAP

72	Palmer Divide	81	Marshall Pass	87	La Veta Pass
73	Ute Pass on Hwy. 24	82	Hayden Pass	88	Cordova Pass
74	Altman's Pass		Town of St. Elmo	89	Cucharas Pass
75	Williams Pass		Towns of Romley and Hancock	90	La Manga Pass
76	Hancock Pass			91	Cumbres Pass
77	Tomichi Pass	83	Medano Pass	92	Raton Pass
78	Black Sage Pass	84	North La Veta Pass		
79	Monarch Pass	85	Pass Creek Pass		
80	Poncha Pass	86	Sangre De Cristo Pass		

141

CONTINENTAL DIVIDE—SOUTHERN COLORADO

72
PALMER DIVIDE

GPS Location: N39° 06' 48" W104° 54' 18"
Elevation: 7,352 feet
First road over top: 1871, the railroad
County: Douglas/El Paso

This low crossing is over a divide called the "Colorado Divide" on a railroad map printed by the Denver and Rio Grande in 1871. The divide separates the drainages of Plum Creek to the north and Monument Creek on the south.

The first people to use this pass were the Plains Indians and the mountain tribes. The first recorded white men to use this trail were members of the United States Army Corps of Engineers. They were led by Major Stephen H. Long, an officer of the army's topographical bureau, commissioned to explore the Rocky Mountains. They arrived in what would later become Denver in July of 1820. Four days later they crossed this divide headed south for Ute Pass at the site of the future Colorado Springs, and then west into South Park.

In the 1830s, the Bean-Sinclair fur trading party followed the Indian trail from today's Colorado Springs to today's Denver. By the 1840s, a trappers trail led from Bent's Fort on the north bank of the Arkansas River midway between today's towns of La Junta and Las Animas to Fort St. Vrain in today's Weld County.

Captain John Fremont left St. Louis in May of 1843 on his second expedition to Colorado. He was looking for routes through the Rocky Mountains that could be used by the military and settlers. He arrived where Denver is now located on July 7, 1843, and camped near Cherry Creek. He went south through today's Castle Rock and crossed over the Black Forest Divide, now named Palmer Divide, to purchase mules and wagons for his men at Pueblo.

On October 27, 1870, General William J. Palmer incorporated his Denver and Rio Grande Railroad Company. His construction crews began grading the road bed and laying ties and rails south out of Denver and up the divide to today's Palmer Lake on the divide. In September of 1871, he built a railroad station next to the lake that he named "Divide." It included a depot, a 50,000-gallon water tank, a boarding house, a livery, and feed stable and maintenance buildings. The rails then continued into Palmer's new town of Colorado Springs. On October 26, 1871, his first passenger train left Denver and five hours later arrived in Colorado Springs. In January of 1884, the divide and the spring-fed natural lake were named Palmer to honor General Palmer. There is a plaque near the summit which reads, "William J. Palmer, Union Cavalry General, Pioneer Railroad Builder who mapped parts of three transcontinental railways and who organized and constructed the Denver and Rio Grande Railroad."

CONTINENTAL DIVIDE—SOUTHERN COLORADO

73
UTE PASS ON HWY. 24

GPS Location: N38° 56' 30" W 105° 09' 27"
Elevation: 9,165 feet
First road over top: 1861
County: Teller
Public access through private land

This pass is an early Indian trail into the mountains from the plains. The Ute Indians came to the hot springs at Manitou, the home of their "Great Spirit," whose breath made the boiling waters bubble. This Indian trail was also used by the Plains Indians (the Comanche, Kiowa, Cheyenne, and Arapaho) to collect game, lodgepoles, salt, and to soak in the healing waters. The pass, first called "Divide," was officially named "Ute Pass" in 1982 by the U.S.G.S. Board on Geographic Names. The watershed divide is at the town of Divide, on the pass' summit at an elevation of 9,165 feet.

In 1842 "Old" Bill Williams was guiding settlers west out of today's Colorado Springs over Ute Pass into South Park and crossed the park to reach the Continental Divide. At the same time Kit Carson was leading trappers into South Park to find beaver. In 1858, prospectors and miners used this old Indian trail to get to South Park's placer mining sites and the Continental Divide's silver and gold hard rock mines.

Colorado City was started in 1859 near today's town of Colorado Springs. In 1860 Colorado City put up $3,000 to upgrade the old Indian trail into a wagon road, which was completed in 1861. In 1862 the officials of the Colorado Territory issued a charter to the Ute Pass Wagon Road Company to build a stagecoach and freight wagon toll road to the top of Ute Pass. In 1872, a wagon road was built up along Fountain Creek, bypassing the old Indian trail above Manitou Springs, to the town of Divide and Ute Pass.

James J. Hagerman had moved to Colorado Springs for the hot springs at Manitou for health reasons. He owned a very rich silver mine near Aspen, and he quickly tired of the high freight costs that the Denver and Rio Grande Railroad charged to move his ore to the smelters. He started his own railway, The Colorado Midland, laying standard gauge rails (4 foot 8 ½ inches wide) to Ute Pass in 1887. He crossed South Park to Trout Creek Pass and the Arkansas River Valley. Rails were laid north to Leadville, then west to the Continental Divide. He used tunnels to go through the Divide to the Frying Pan River and Aspen Junction, and south up the Roaring Fork River into Aspen.

CONTINENTAL DIVIDE—SOUTHERN COLORADO

74
ALTMAN'S PASS

GPS Location: N 38° 44' 10" W 105° 08' 02"
Elevation: 11,940 feet
County: Chaffee/Gunnison
Gunnison/San Isabel National Forest
On the divide
No road over top

This pass was discovered by Colonel Henry A. Altman early in 1880. It is reported that he was looking for a stagecoach route that would connect the town of St. Elmo on the east side of the Continental Divide with the town of Pitkin on the west side of the divide.

Altman heard that the Denver, South Park and Pacific Railroad was planning to bore a tunnel near the top of the divide for their transcontinental railway. He contacted James A. Evans, the locating and construction engineer of the South Park Railroad, about using his stagecoach route for their tunnel and railway. Dr. John Evans, the ex-Governor of Colorado, was the president of the South Park's board of directors who decided to use Altman's trail for their tunnel route. It is probable that Altman helped locate and build the first tunnel through the Continental Divide.

The South Park rails were laid into St. Elmo in December of 1880. Evans started boring his Alpine tunnel two miles above Romley. His tunnel elevation sloped from 11,608 feet to 11,546 feet to allow water to drain out of the tunnel. He had hoped to find solid granite when he started boring, but instead found decomposed granite, loose rock, and seeping water. It became necessary to line the ceiling and side walls with California redwood to seal out the water. Rails were laid and the first train ran through the first railroad tunnel in the Continental Divide in June of 1882. The rail line was abandoned in 1910. Altman's trail and the west portal are four miles south of Tincup Pass as the eagle flies.

CONTINENTAL DIVIDE—SOUTHERN COLORADO

The upper road was the railroad right-of-way below the palisades. The lower diagonal road is the early Williams Pass road used to move men and materials for boring the Alpine Tunnel.

75
WILLIAMS PASS

GPS Location: N 38° 38' 30" W 106° 23' 22"
Elevation: 11,766 feet
First road over top: 1880
County: Chaffee/Gunnison
Gunnison/San Isabel National Forest
On the Continental Divide
Pass requires high clearance four wheel drive vehicle

We do not know the names of the first white men who crossed the Continental Divide using the pass called "Williams." It was one of several passes on the divide from the town of Pitkin on the west side of the Divide to Hancock and St. Elmo on the east side. It was reported that in the mid-1840s, the master trapper, fur trader, and guide William S. Williams used this crossing. He was called "Old" to show respect for him; he was a mountain man's mountain man.

Today's Williams Pass road.

We also do not know who built the first wagon road over the pass called "Williams." We do know that it was used by prospectors in 1880. Robert R. Williams, Assistant Construction Engineer for the Denver and South Park Railroad suggested using the existing Williams Pass road as a supply road for moving the men and materials needed to bore the Alpine Tunnel. Freight wagons were using the upgraded Williams Wagon road to the east portal of the tunnel, then over the pass to the west portal by November of 1880.

The South Park's construction crews chose to use the Williams Road on the west side of the divide for building their rails. Two miles from the west portal, they built sculpted rock walls, backfilling them with loose rocks to build a road bed at the necessary grade levels. This engineering feat is called "The Palisades."

My wife Laurel and I walked on the Williams Pass road in the summer of 2012. The road is loose rocks called a scree-field. It was obvious that no maintenance had been done on the road since 1882.

CONTINENTAL DIVIDE—SOUTHERN COLORADO

76
HANCOCK PASS

GPS Location: N 38° 37' 15" W 106° 22' 27"
Elevation: 12,120 Feet
First road over top: Late 1880s
County: Chaffee/Gunnison
Gunnison/San Isabel National Forest
On the Continental Divide
Pass requires high clearance four wheel drive vehicle

This road to the Continental Divide's east side begins at today's town of Nathrop on the Arkansas River. The road heads west upstream along Chalk Creek, passing the Mt. Princeton Hot Springs, another one of the Ute Indian's healing places. The road then continues past the townsites of Alpine and Iron City and the town of St. Elmo. At St. Elmo the road heads south through the town of Romley and up to the townsite of Hancock.

It was at Hancock that the Denver and South Park Railroad started the steep climb to the east portal of their Alpine Tunnel. The elevation of the town of Hancock

The Mary Murphy tram towers by Cindy Williams.

CONTINENTAL DIVIDE—SOUTHERN COLORADO

Just past the townsite of Hancock is the start of the exciting section of the Hancock Pass road.

is 11,027 feet and the short road to the pass summit is above timberline. The pass road crosses the Continental Divide one-half mile east of Williams Pass. From the top of the Divide the road down the west side crosses today's Brittle Silver Basin to follow Middle Quartz Creek to its junction with North Quartz Creek northeast of the town of Pitkin.

77
TOMICHI PASS

GPS Location: N 38° 36' 13" W 106° 23' 00"
Elevation: 11,979 feet
First road over top: 1880
County: Gunnison
Gunnison National Forest
Pass requires high clearance four wheel drive vehicle

In 1876 prospectors from the Arkansas River Valley traveled west up Chalk Creek to use today's Hancock Pass over the Continental Divide. From the pass summit, they worked their way down to the headwaters of Tomichi Creek. Tomichi is the Ute Indian word for "hot water." The first mining camp built on the creek was Glenwood in early May of 1880. The town of Tomichi was platted in late May of 1880. By 1882 over 1,200 miners were working in the Tomichi Mining District. The two mines that were the greatest silver ore producers were the Magna Charta Tunnel in 1881 and the Legal Tender in 1883. Two other mining camps were built downstream from the town of Tomichi. They were the towns of North Star two miles west of the Continental Divide and the town of Whitepine. Winter avalanches and fires destroyed the town of Tomichi in 1899.

To the north of Tomichi and Whitepine, a high ridge blocks the way into Brittle Silver Basin. It has a saddle at a point just below 12,000 feet that the road crossed and today we call it "Tomichi Pass." Today's Forest Road 888 is the road that crosses Tomichi Pass. It continues on the steep side of Brittle Silver Basin to Middle Quartz Creek and Quartz Creek down to the town of Pitkin. Travelers from Whitepine could head downstream along Tomichi Creek to use Black Sage Pass to Waunita Hot Springs and Waunita Pass into Pitkin. From Pitkin they would ride through Ohio City and Parlin, and into the town of Gunnison.

78
BLACK SAGE PASS

GPS Location: N 38° 29' 26" W 106° 27' 06
Elevation: 9,745 feet
First road over top: Late 1870s
County: Gunnison
Gunnison National Forest

The Black Sage Pass Road used an Indian trail to provide a lower crossing from the Arkansas River Valley to Pitkin on the west side of the Continental Divide. The prospectors used what is now called "Old Monarch Pass" to cross the divide. Next they went west into the Tomichi Valley to cross Black Sage Pass to the Waunita Hot Springs and Waunita Pass to the town of Pitkin.

The name Black Sage describes a variant color for sagebrush usually seen with gray-green leaves. The first white men to use this pass was the Hayden surveying party in 1874-'75 measuring and mapping the mountains, rivers, and valleys. The first wagon road over Black Sage was built in the late 1870s.

In 1880, freight wagons and stage coaches regularly crossed from the mining district of White Pine to the town of Pitkin. The pass road crosses a low divide three miles east of the Tomichi dome and three miles north of Quakey Mountain.

CONTINENTAL DIVIDE—SOUTHERN COLORADO

The Madonna Mine dominates the landscape on the east side of Monarch Pass. Because of the limestone content, the ore was shipped to Pueblo to be used as a flux in the iron making process.

79
MONARCH PASS

GPS Location: N 38° 29' 48" W 106° 19' 32"
Elevation: 11,312 feet
First road over top: 1880
County: Chaffee/Gunnison
Gunnison/San Isabel National Forest
On the Continental Divide

In 1887 Nicholas Creede discovered silver on the east side of the Continental Divide at this pass. His mines were named "The Little Charm" and the "Monarch." The dictionary definition of monarch is "a person who rules over a kingdom or empire." Creede probably named his mine Monarch because of its quality and quantity of silver.

A wagon road was built over this pass by the Boone brothers in 1880. Their road crossed the pass at the elevation of 11,525 feet. A stagecoach line crossed here to reach the Gunnison River Valley. General Ulysses Grant crossed Monarch Pass on his tour of mining towns. Today this road is called the "Original Monarch Pass Road."

CONTINENTAL DIVIDE—SOUTHERN COLORADO

The Colorado Highway Department built a new crossing one mile south and 150 feet lower than the original pass road. The altitude of this second pass is 11,375 feet. A lower pass meant less problems with blizzards and avalanches closing the highway. The new road was built for automobile use, but it was only a graveled road. Today this road over Monarch Pass is called "The Old Monarch Pass Road." The road was a section of the cross-country "Rainbow Route."

In 1939, a third pass crossing was built one-half mile east and 60 feet lower than Old Monarch, at the elevation of 11,312 feet. This new crossing was chosen by Charles D. Vail, the Chief Engineer of the Colorado Department of Highways.

Today's Monarch Pass Road heads west out of Poncha Springs and passes through Maysville, Garfield, and Monarch next to the south fork of the Arkansas River. It reaches the summit of the pass near the Madonna Mine and Limestone Quarry. After crossing the Monarch Road summit, the Monarch Road follows Agate Creek down stream to its junction with Tomichi Creek. In November of 1939, the Highway Department opened this new twenty-eight mile stretch of U.S. 50 for traffic.

80
PONCHA PASS

GPS Location: N 38°25' 20" W 106° 05' 13"
Elevation: 9,010 feet
Road over top: 1867
County: Chaffee/Saguache
Public access through private land

Recorded history gives credit to Mexico's Governor Juan Bautista De Anza for naming this pass. He had come north from Santa Fe to find and destroy Chief Cuerno Verde's renegade Comanche Indians, who had been raiding Spanish colonists in northern New Mexico. De Anza entered the south end of the San Luis Valley and traveled north with the San Juan Mountains on his left and the Sangre de Cristos on his right. On August 27, 1779, he crossed this pass and named it Poncha, the Spanish word for "mild." Poncha is a twenty mile-wide saddle on the Sangre de Cristos which separates the waters of the Rio Grande River from the waters of the Upper Arkansas River.

De Anza's soldiers followed the Comanche's trail around the west side of Pike's Peak and trapped them near Fountain Creek, twenty-five miles east of today's Ute Pass. On August 31, De Anza's army attacked and killed eighteen Comanche warriors and thirty-four women and children. Sometime prior to this battle Chief Verde had led 200 of his warriors south to raid Taos. De Anza's men followed Chief Verde's trail and caught up with him near today's Greenhorn Mountain in the Wet Mountain Range. This second battle with the Comanches resulted in the death of Cuerno Verde, his sons, and many of the Indian warriors. It put an end to Comanche raiding in the northern New Mexico mountains.

CONTINENTAL DIVIDE—SOUTHERN COLORADO

Heading north past Villa Grove on Highway 285, the Poncha Pass road exits the San Luis Valley over the distant pass and into Poncha Springs.

In June of 1853, Captain John W. Gunnison led a U.S. Congress approved railroad survey expedition from Kansas City to find a railroad route to Salt Lake City. He crossed the Sangre de Cristos to camp at Saguache. On August 29, he led his men northwest to look at Poncha Pass for a railroad route. He didn't like what he saw, returned to Saguache, and headed northwest to cross the Continental Divide using Cochetopa Pass. Gunnison's team continued northwesterly to the river, now bearing his name, until it met the Uncompahgre River. From there the river flows north to meet the Colorado at Grand Junction and heads west into Utah.

A young store owner in the town of Saguache needed a road to bring him supplies. He was encouraged to build a toll road. Otto Mears bought his first road charter on November 8, 1870. He surveyed and built his road north through Villa Grove and across Poncha Pass, which is three miles east of the Continental Divide. He ended his fifty mile road at Nathrop in the Arkansas River Valley. The Poncha Pass wagon road is part of U.S. Highway 285.

81
MARSHALL PASS

GPS Location: N 38° 23' 29" W 106° 14' 50"
Elevation: 10,846 feet
First road over top: 1877
County: Saguache
Gunnison/San Isabel National Forest
On the Continental Divide

Lt. George Wheeler's U.S. Army surveyors were mapping the San Juans in 1873 when one of his crew, Lt. Wm. L. Marshall, came down with a severe toothache. He and a friend chose the fastest of the mules and started over Cinnamon Pass to the future site of Lake City and Cochetopa Pass. He didn't want to have to cross the San Luis Valley

CONTINENTAL DIVIDE—SOUTHERN COLORADO

and the Sangre De Cristos so he started north and crossed the pass now named Marshall, and went down to the Arkansas Valley. He headed northeast and finally found a real dentist in Denver. His discovery of Marshall Pass saved him 125 miles of trail and four days of toothache.

Otto Mears incorporated his Poncha, Marshall, and Gunnison Toll Road on April 14, 1879. Construction started at Poncha Springs following Poncha Creek to Mears' Junction, where it headed west to cross Marshall Pass on the Continental Divide. The road down from the pass followed Marshall Creek to today's town of Sargents. It then followed Tomichi Creek to today's Parlin and Gunnison. Mears built his sixty mile toll road in 1879-1880.

In October of 1880 General William J. Palmer sent his railroad surveyors north from Salida to cross over Poncha Pass heading west to today's Gunnison. They followed the Marshall Pass Toll Road which Palmer bought from Otto Mears. The railroad construction crew crossed Marshall's "Toothache Pass" by June 21, 1881 and continued west into Gunnison. On August 8, 1881, the first Denver and Rio Grande train of two coal cars, a baggage car, two passenger cars, and a caboose whistled into Gunnison.

The railroad station on top of Marshall pass had a post office until 1952. The Denver and Rio Grande stopped operation in 1953 and the rails were removed in 1955.

82
HAYDEN PASS

GPS Location: N 38° 17' 35" W 105° 51' 02"
Elevation: 11,184 feet
First road over top: 1880s
County: Fremont/Saguache
San Isabel/ Rio Grande National Forest
Pass requires high clearance four wheel drive vehicle

The Hayden Pass was not named for Dr. Ferdinand V. Hayden. The U.S. Forest Service recorded that the pass was named for Lewis Hayden, a rancher from Texas living in the Wet Mountain Valley on the east side of the Sangre de Cristo Mountains.

The pass was first used by the Ute Indians to cross the Sangre de Cristo Mountains. Dr. Hayden's surveyors measured and mapped the Sangre de Cristo Mountains. Dr. Hayden showed Hayden's Pass in the 1877 Atlas of Colorado that he published when he finished his Rocky Mountain surveying assignment.

The Hayden Pass road is located at the north end of the San Luis Valley. The pass road starts at today's town of Coaldale on the east slope of the Sangre de Cristos. From there the road climbs upstream to the pass along a creek now named Hayden. From the pass the road heads west downstream along the Hayden Pass Creek to the town of Villa Grove.

CONTINENTAL DIVIDE—SOUTHERN COLORADO

TOWN OF ST. ELMO

John Royal and the medical doctor Abner E. Wright were among the first miners to ascend Chalk Creek from the Arkansas River Valley. Together they discovered the Mary Murphy Mine on Chrysolite Mountain above Romley in 1875. In 1878 Wright sold his share of the mine and moved into Buena Vista to practice medicine.

In 1878, a rancher named William W. Campbell started his ranch on the future site of St. Elmo. He built one of the first homes in the town first named Forest City. Because there was a town with that name in California, the postoffice made this new town change its name. They borrowed their name from a novel written by Augusta J. Evans, whose hero was St. Elmo Murray. The town of St. Elmo was incorporated on October 15, 1880.

In 1870, miners working at the Mary Murphy Mine organized The Mt. Princeton Hot Springs and Improvement Company and opened it for public use. On November 15, 1913, The Mt. Princeton Hot Springs was incorporated by new owners called the Carlsbad Hot Springs Corporation. Financial problems caused the corporation to sell the hot springs to a Kansas City millionaire named J. C. Gifford on December 8, 1915. He built a fantastic hotel above the springs to house guests from all over the United States.

Several of the Continental Divide passes start or end near St. Elmo. The passes are Williams, Hancock, and Tincup. Stage and freight service to the mining town of Tincup used the Chalk Creek and Elk Mountain Toll Road over the Divide. The road headed west along the North Fork of Chalk Creek to the pass, then followed East Willow Creek to Mirror Lake and into Tincup.

In the early 1860s, Anton and Anna Stark moved to St. Elmo from Hayes, Kansas. Anton worked for the South Park Railroad and Anna operated their Home Comfort Hotel. Their children, Annabell, Tony, and Roy were among the last residents of St. Elmo. The post office was closed in 1952 and the county stopped plowing the road in the winter. When Annabelle died in 1960, the Stark era of five decades ended.

In 1967 Doyle and Pricella Hartman bought the St. Elmo Trading Post to run a grocery store. The building was not originally built in St. Elmo. It was moved into town, probably from Hancock. Pricella ran the store until it burned to the ground. Pricella Hartman bought the "Mongrain Building" in 1881. The ground floor housed a small general store and the restaurant named "The Pack Saddle," which was operated by B. J. Smith and Pricella Hartman. There were many families visiting and living in St. Elmo in the summers, enjoying the beauty and seclusion and most were active in the preservation of the town.

In 1890, a major fire destroyed most of the south side of St. Elmo's main street. The fire was reported to have started in either the Clifton Hotel or the jewelry store. It burned the postoffice, a butcher shop, the Clifton Hotel, a bakery, a shoe store, and warehouses. None of these buildings were rebuilt.

The last Denver, South Park and Pacific train went through the Alpine Tunnel in 1910 and the tunnel was abandoned. The Mary Murphy Mine above the town of Romley was a major producer of silver and gold until 1917. When the railroad ended and the mines closed permanently, St. Elmo hibernated.

CONTINENTAL DIVIDE—SOUTHERN COLORADO

Lee Kerrison visited St. Elmo for the first time in the summer of 1970 and started living there in the summer of 1971. He bought property in 1973, built a cabin on it, and still owns it. In January of 1980 he bought the original Miners Exchange Building which at one time housed one of Pat Hurley's saloons. He used the building for his home and a full blown grocery store and still does. In 1984, he was awarded a jeep rental permit to be used in and around St. Elmo. In 1995, Lee's son Chris and daughter-in-law Lois Connell became his partners in the ownership and operation of the General Store and the ATV Rentals of St. Elmo. Lee is also an antique dealer out of his store. In the last fifty years police protection in St. Elmo was provided by the Chaffee County Sheriff. Fire protection is provided by a station in Nathrop operated by the Chaffee County Fire Department. Lee is still St. Elmo's historian and preservationist!

TOWNS OF ROMLEY AND HANCOCK

Romley was a mining town in the mid-1870s four miles up Chalk Creek from St. Elmo. Its reason for existence was the discovery of the Mary Murphy Mine by John Royal and A. E. Wright in 1875. Mary Murphy was a Denver nurse who cared for Royal during a lengthy illness. By 1883, the Mary Murphy vein produced as much as 2,000 tons of gold and silver ore a month. Most of the ore came from one vein that was 5 feet wide, almost 300 feet long, and 800 feet deep. The mine's air compressors, ore house, mill, and company offices were located at Romley. The Pat Murphy Mine on the north slope of Chrysolite Mountain was an underground continuation of the Mary Murphy Mine.

The mines used a tramway to move ore down to be shipped to smelters and mills. The tramway was an overhead endless cable supported on fifty towers approximately eighty feet apart. Each of the ninety-six buckets could carry 2,000 pounds of ore, moving 128 tons of ore in twenty hours. The tramway was operated by two men and made a complete round trip in forty minutes. The tram was a gravity tram carrying ore down and timbers up to the mine.

The town of Hancock was five miles south of St. Elmo. The first miners arrived in 1880. The town was built at the elevation of 11,027 feet, which made living and working in Hancock's winters difficult and dangerous. When the South Park Railroad started building their Alpine Tunnel through the Continental Divide, Hancock became a railroad station. Deep snow at both of the tunnel's portals in 1890 ended the railroad and the town of Hancock. The tunnel was reopened in 1895 then permanently abandoned in 1917.

In 1927, the Mary Murphy Mine went into receivership and remained there until 1972. During this time various individuals leased portions of the property, but their efforts at mining failed.

CONTINENTAL DIVIDE—SOUTHERN COLORADO

83
MEDANO PASS

GPS Location: N 37° 51' 22" W 105° 25' 58"
Elevation: 10,030 feet
First road over top: unknown
County: Huerfano/Saguache
Rio Grande/San Isabel National Forest
Pass requires high clearance four wheel drive vehicle

The Comanche Indians in south-central Colorado were terrorists—stealing horses, enslaving other Indians, and killing white settlers. Led by Cuerno Verde (Green Horn) they started raiding along the Rio Grande River. In August of 1779 Governor Juan Bautista De Anza left Santa Fe with soldiers and settlers to end the Comanche raiding. They surprised the Comanches at Fountain Creek west of today's Colorado Springs on August 31 and destroyed their village. Verde and 200 warriors were not in camp; they were headed to raid Taos New Mexico. De Anza chased and caught up with Verde's

This photograph shows one of the many creek crossings that can become very deep depending on the time of year.

When descending the west side of the pass, the road becomes sandier until the road base is total deep sand. This road ends in the Great Sand Dunes National Park.

warriors, killing most of them. Returning home he crossed and named the Sangre de Cristo Mountains and its main pass "Medano," Spanish for "sand hill."

The Medano Pass Road starts at the townsite of Bradford south of today's town of Westcliffe. It climbs west for twelve miles to the pass summit. From the summit the road down follows Medano Creek for ten miles to the Great Sand Dunes. Many years ago the valley floor was covered with a large lake that receded and drained dry, leaving behind a thick sand sheet. Gradually the sand was picked up by the southwest winds and blown towards a low area of the Sangre de Cristo Mountain Range. The sand was funneled toward three passes: Mosca, Medano, and Music. Strong winter storms would blow the sand back into the San Luis Valley and dump it, causing the dunes to grow vertically. Two mountain streams, Medano and Sand Creek, also carried sand back to the valley floor.

Army Lt. Zebulon Pike was given orders on June 24, 1806, to lead an expedition to explore Colorado's Arkansas River to its headwaters. Pike's party arrived in Colorado in November of 1806. In January of 1807, they crossed a mountain pass which Pike named "Pike's Gap." The Spaniards had called this pass "Medano," its proper name today.

CONTINENTAL DIVIDE—SOUTHERN COLORADO

The Medano Pass Crossing had been used by trappers and traders heading south from Bent's Fort on the Arkansas River to Taos. When Lt. John Fremont, guided by Kit Carson, saw Medano Pass in June of 1842, he said that the pass would not work for a stagecoach route because the sand would choke the west end. Since then a drivable road has been built on the west side of the dunes.

In March of 1853, the United States Congress approved a railroad survey to find the best route for a railroad through the Colorado Rockies. Captain John W. Gunnison led an expedition from today's Kansas City on June 23, 1853, to find a railroad route. They reached Bent's Fort in August and crossed Medano Pass. They chose to continue their search for a railroad and crossed the San Luis Valley into today's Gunnison River Valley.

84
NORTH LA VETA PASS

GPS Location: N 37° 36' 48" W 105° 11' 27"
Elevation: 9,413 feet
First road over top: 1963
County: Costilla/Huerfano
Public access through private land

The Denver and Rio Grande Railroad ownership decided to stop using narrow gauge rails across the Sangre de Cristo Mountains in 1890. They surveyed and selected a new lower elevation crossing for their standard gauge rails. This new route left the town of La Veta headed west up Middle Creek to a pass at the elevation of 9,242 feet that they named "Veta." Next the railway was graded and rails laid downstream along Wagon Creek to today's Fort Garland and Alamosa.

The new standard gauge railroad was completed and opened in 1899. Years later the rails on La Veta Pass were removed and the La Veta route was upgraded to wagon road status. With the arrival of the automobile, La Veta was upgraded to a graveled road. In the 1960s the Colorado Highway Department surveyed a route to build a new paved road north of La Veta Pass. This road was built in the summers of 1961-62, opened for traffic in 1963, and is a section of U.S. Highway 160. This new pass is named North La Veta Pass. "Veta" is the Spanish word translated as "vein." It was chosen because of the white mineral surface veins north of the town of La Veta.

CONTINENTAL DIVIDE—SOUTHERN COLORADO

85
PASS CREEK PASS

GPS Location: N 37° 37' 14" W 105° 13' 46"
Elevation: 9,380 feet
First road over top: early 1850s
County: Costilla/Huerfano
Public access through private land

The Pass Creek road started near the top of the Sangre De Cristo Pass road headed north in the Sangre de Cristo Mountains. The first name used for this road that ends in today's Gardner was "Ute." We do not know who named the road and its pass "Pass Creek." There are legends that tell us that the first people to use this road were the Spanish explorers and miners working in Pass Creek Canyon. It is reported that there is a rock in the canyon with the autograph of Jean L. Archeveque carved in the early 1700s.

The old Ute trail brought Tom Sharp to Pass Creek in the late 1860s. He was a merchant and stock raiser who built a trading post on the north side of the Huerfano River. He was acquainted with and did business with Chief Ouray and the Utes. Trappers and traders from Santa Fe and Taos, New Mexico, used this trail to sell items from Taos to settlers near Hardscrabble. This low pass was a good choice for the wagon road built over it in the early 1850s. It was used to supply Forts Garland and Massachusetts on the east side of the San Luis Valley.

The Pass Creek road starts on today's U.S. 160 about two miles west of the North La Veta Pass summit. The road runs alongside Sheep Mountain and Little Sheep Mountain in the Huerfano River Valley and ends in the town of Gardner.

86
SANGRE DE CRISTO PASS

GPS Location: N 37° 37' 10" W 105° 11' 42"
Elevation: 9,468 feet
First road over top: September 1779
County: Costillo/Huerfano
On Private Land
No road over top today

In the spring of 1833, William and Charles Bent and Ceran St. Vrain built a trading post on the north bank of the Arkansas River near today's town of La Junta. They planned to trade supplies with the fur trappers and the Cheyenne and Arapaho Indians. This was the starting point of the "Trappers Trail" that followed the Huerfano River to a low natural opening in today's Sangre de Cristo Mountains. After reaching

CONTINENTAL DIVIDE—SOUTHERN COLORADO

today's Sangre de Cristo Pass, the Trapper's Trail entered the San Luis Valley and continued to Taos, New Mexico.

In 1777, Juan Bautista de Anza was chosen to be the Governor of New Mexico. His first assignment was to capture the Comanche Indians in Southern Colorado who were attacking Mexican citizens and Ute Indians. In two major battles Anza destroyed their Chief Cuervo Verde and ended the Comanche raiding. On their return trip to New Mexico the Spaniards camped on a spruce covered pass. When the sun set on the peaks around them it turned them red with an alpen glow. He named the pass "Sangre de Cristo," Spanish for the "Blood of Christ."

The pass was regularly used by buffalo going from the San Luis Valley to the Great Plains, and it was traveled by the Ute Indians chasing the buffalo for food and clothing. In 1853, Captain John W. Gunnison led a topography expedition to find a railroad route. His plan was to use Sangre de Cristo Pass over the Sangre De Cristo Mountains into the San Luis Valley and Cochetopa Pass into today's Gunnison River Valley. When he arrived at the Sangre de Cristo Mountains, Gunnison decided that the old Spanish trail up South Oak Creek was too rocky for his wagons. He built a six-mile wagon road to the pass to continue his westward journey in August of 1853.

A wagon road was established over Sangre de Cristo by the U.S. Army to provide a supply and mail route to Fort Garland. In 1866, the Army built Fort Stevens to protect the mail routes. One branch of the Santa Fe Trail followed the Arkansas River to the Huerfano River and crossed Sangre de Cristo Pass. The Mosca Pass Toll Road was in operation from the 1870s to 1905. It was the Denver and Rio Grande's Railroad crossing of La Veta Pass that ended the use of Sangre de Cristo Pass. The pass road is no longer open for the public, both ends of the pass road are closed by private property.

87

LA VETA PASS

GPS Location: N 37° 04' 39" W 106° 23' 10"
Elevation: 9,382 feet
First road over top: 1870
County: Costilla/Huerfano
Public Access through private land

The first good wagon road to cross the Sangre de Cristo Mountains from the east was built by the Cucharas and Sangre De Cristo Wagon Road Company. On June 15, 1868, they were chartered to build their road. Construction started on the route at the Francisco homestead in today's town of La Veta. The road was built upstream along South Abeyta Creek and crossed a saddle which the railroad later called "Veta Pass." The road continued downstream along today's Sangre De Cristo Creek to the San Luis Valley. The Abeyta Pass Toll Road Company was incorporated on December 15, 1873, to improve the early Sangre De Cristo Road. They called their new road the Abeyta Pass Toll Road.

CONTINENTAL DIVIDE—SOUTHERN COLORADO

General William J. Palmer was the founder and owner of the Denver and Rio Grande Railroad. He was a professional railroad builder trained by J. Edgar Thomson in Pennsylvania. By 1876 Palmer had built 200 miles of rails from Denver through Colorado Springs to Trinidad. He changed his original plan of building to the lower Rio Grande River in Texas and made plans to build west into the San Luis Valley and beyond. He built three-foot gauge rails west from Walsenburg along the Cucharas River to today's town of La Veta at the confluence of the Cucharas River with the South Abeyta Creek in 1876. La Veta was a railroad station that included a section house, bunkhouse, turntable for a roundhouse, maintenance building, machine shop, coal house, carpenter shop, and a depot. The station was a "helper" station with extra locomotives ready to help trains over the steep mountains.

In the spring of 1877, Palmer built his rails upstream along South Abeyta Creek to the foot of Dump Mountain. He used a muleshoe curve on the mountain's east side with rails doubling back over themselves to reach the summit of Veta Pass at the elevation of 9,382 feet. Palmer's railroad was the first one built across a Rocky Mountain range.

The Denver and Rio Grande built a station on the pass summit with a bunkhouse, depot, section house, coal house, coal platform, and a fifty foot turntable. After crossing the pass, rails were built downstream along Sangre de Cristo Creek to today's town of Russell. Russell was a helper station with a roundhouse, coal house, and water tank. The rails continued west from Russell through Fort Garland and today's town of Blanca and into Alamosa in 1878.

The Denver and Rio Grande hired civil engineer R.L. Kelly to determine the wisdom of installing four foot eight and one-half inch standard gauge rails over Veta Pass. His surveys showed that it would be too costly, so the D&RG abandoned that route. The railroad still needed to be able to use and connect with standard gauge railroads. Surveyors located a new twenty-seven mile route in 1898 from the town of La Veta to cross the Sangre de Cristo Mountains and run down to Russell in the San Luis Valley. This route was seven miles south of Veta Pass and due west of the town of La Veta. The D&RG construction crews graded the new route in 7½ months and spiked down the rails in 1½ months. This new pass summit was at the elevation of 9,242 feet, 140 feet lower than the narrow gauge summit. The last narrow gauge train over the old Veta Pass was on August 27, 1899, and the rails were removed in 1902. The first passenger train over the new standard gauge rails was on November 12, 1899. The railroad owners named this new road and pass "Veta."

When the narrow gauge rails were removed

The D&RG depot was built in 1877 and still stands at the summit.

from Dump Mountain, their right-of-way was used to build a wagon road. In 1916 the Colorado Highway Department improved this road for automobile travel. It appears that the name La Veta was given to this road and its pass at this time, probably because it begins at the town of La Veta.

In the early 1960s the highway department built a new paved road about 1½ miles north of the La Veta Road. It was at a lower altitude and more direct than the La Veta Road and was named "North La Veta Pass."

In 1870, W.T. Sharp opened a trading post named Buzzard Roost Ranch along Pass Creek near the old copper mining town of Malachite. Some of his regular customers were Chief Ouray's Utes coming from their camps near Sheep Mountain. Tom Sharp and Ouray became friends. It is reported that Ouray and his wife Chipeta rode the D&RG's narrow gauge over Veta Pass.

Charles Darwin sent Alfred Wallace, Sir Joseph Hooker, and Asa Gray to investigate Rocky Mountain's botanicals. He thought that flowers found in the Sangre de Cristos near La Veta could validate his theory of evolution written in his book *On the Origin of Species*. The men could have used the D&RG to reach their goal by crossing Veta Pass.

88
CORDOVA PASS

GPS Location: N 37° 20' 55" W 105° 01' 30"
Elevation: 11,248 feet
First road over top: 1935
County: Huerfano/Los Animas
San Isabel National Forest

The Cordova Pass road starts at the summit of Cucharas Pass. About six miles northeast, the road crosses Cordova Pass on the ridge that connects Cucharas Pass to West Spanish Peak. The pass was originally called Apishapa, the Apache word for stinking water, which describes pools of stagnant water next to the road at the foot of the pass.

Just a few miles east of Apishapa Pass the pass road reached an igneous rock dike. The road builders bored a tunnel through the dike and named it the Apishapa Arch. The thirty-six mile road continued through the townsite of Gulnare and ends in the town of Aguilar.

Dikes were formed when magma, molten rock material from inside the earth, was forced up through cracks in the sedimentary material on the earth's surface. When the surface material eroded, hard rock walls remained. Today dikes radiate out from West and East Spanish Peaks like spokes on a wagon wheel. The dikes are from one to 100 feet wide and are up to 1/4 miles long. The terminus of the Cucharas Pass road is named Stonewall because of the many dikes nearby.

The Cordova Pass road was built by Huerfano and Las Animas counties using men from the Works Progress Administration (W.P.A) and The Civilian Conservation

CONTINENTAL DIVIDE—SOUTHERN COLORADO

This area is unique for its igneous dikes that radiate outward from the Spanish Peaks. The Cordova road builders tunneled a dike and called it the Apishapa Dike.

Corps (C.C.C.). Apishapa Pass became Cordova Pass when the W.P.A. finished building the automobile road in 1935. It was renamed Cordova to honor the County Commissioner J.J. Cordova, who worked long and hard to make the road happen.

89
CUCHARAS PASS

GPS Location: N 37° 20' 25" W 104° 59' 54"
Elevation: 9,995 feet
First road over top: 1706
County: Huerfano/Los Animas
San Isabel National Forest

The Cucharas Pass road starts at the town of Cuchara and ends at the town of Stonewall. The name "Cucharas" is Spanish for "spoon," probably used to describe the shape of the valley on the north side of the pass. The ridge that the pass straddles divides the waters of the Cucharas River from the waters of the Purgatoire River. After crossing the pass, the road runs down around North Lake and Monument Lake to the town of Stonewall.

CONTINENTAL DIVIDE—SOUTHERN COLORADO

Marshall Sprague, the godfather of pass historians, wrote that the first Spanish explorers in the area were led by Captain Juan De Ulibarri in 1706. He left Santa Fe with 140 soldiers to stop renegade Apache Indians from capturing settlers and stealing horses in the Sangre de Cristo Mountains. He was successful and crossed Cucharas Pass in the summer of 1706. In August of 1779 Governor Juan Bautista De Anza crossed Cucharas Pass on his way back to New Mexico after defeating the Comanche Indians south of today's Colorado Springs. The fertile valleys on both ends of the pass road were settled by potato farmers and stock-raisers in the 1880s. It is recorded that Henry Daigre hired Hiram Vasquez to improve the pass trail to a good wagon road in 1865. George Mears moved his family into the Cucharas Valley for health reasons. He opened a resort and named it "Cuchara Camps." The valley became a summer playground for mid-westerners.

90
LA MANGA PASS

GPS Location: N 37° 04' 39" W 106° 23' 10"
Elevation: 10,230 feet
First road over top: mid 1920s
County: Conejos
Rio Grande National Forest

To some early explorers this pass must have looked like a coat sleeve, so they named it "La Manga." La Manga Pass crosses a low divide between the North Fork of the "Rio (river) De Los Piños" and the creek named "La Manga."

The Denver and Rio Grande Railroad laid fifteen miles of rails from the town of Alamosa to the town of Antonito. Rails were spiked down west out of Antonito to a new railroad station named Los Piños. They continued laying rails to cross over Cumbres Pass and through New Mexico's Toltec Canon to Chama, New Mexico.

In the 1920s, the Colorado Highway Department built a new highway from Antonito to Chama, naming it State Highway 17. It was constructed due west through the small town of Fox Creek in the Conejos River Valley. At La Manga Creek the road was built upstream to cross La Manga Pass. From the pass summit, State Highway 17 followed the Denver and Rio Grande Railway into New Mexico and the town of Chama.

No town existed at La Manga Pass in this farming and ranching area, and the railroad never crossed La Manga Pass.

CONTINENTAL DIVIDE—SOUTHERN COLORADO

The picture is of the railroad's depot on Cumbres Pass.

91
CUMBRES PASS

GPS Location: N 37° 01' 14" W 106° 27' 00"
First road over top: 1879
Elevation: 10,022 feet
County: Conejos
Rio Grande National Forest

There are two mountain passes to be crossed between the town of Antonita, Colorado and the New Mexico border. The first is La Manga and the second is Cumbres. The word "Cumbres" is Spanish for "crest." Cumbres Pass is about eleven miles east of the Continental Divide and two and one-half miles north of the New Mexico border.

In 1858, military units from Fort Garland in the San Luis Valley traveled westward across Cumbres to Fort Lewis at today's Pagosa Springs. During the summer of 1874, one division of the Hayden Survey Party explored the southern Colorado Summitville Mining District to measure and map the mountains. They discovered the passes now named La Manga, Railroad, Summit, Elwood, and Cumbres. A toll road was built over Cumbres Pass in the summer of 1879.

In 1880, the Denver and Rio Grande Railroad started building its San Juan Division out of the town of Alamosa. They graded the road bed and spiked down the rails south to Antonito. They continued the rails over Cumbres Pass to and through the Toltec Canyon into Chama, New Mexico. They arrived in Chama on February 1, 1881. In the summer of 1881, the rails were laid northwest into Durango. Durango is one of the many towns started by the Denver and Rio Grande. They called their buildings a railroad "station." A station included a depot, the siding yard, maintenance buildings, a roundhouse, water tower, wood and coal storage areas, and employee housing.

In the early 1920s, a modern graveled road was built over Cumbres. In 1970, the states of New Mexico and Colorado bought the railway from Antonito to Chama and began joint operation of today's Cumbres and Toltec Scenic Railroad. The railroad is the longest and highest narrow gauge railroad in North America. It is also the only operational railroad in Colorado that crosses a mountain pass.

92
RATON PASS

GPS Location: N 36° 59' 28" W 104° 29' 12"
Elevation: 7,881 feet
First road over top: 1821
County: Los Animas
Public access through private land

There is a mountain pass on the Colorado/New Mexico border where today's Interstate Highway 25 crosses a low mountain range. The pass is called Raton, Spanish for "mouse or packrat." Captain William Becknell constructed the "Mountain Branch" of the Santa Fe Trail across Raton Pass. The Santa Fe Trail started on the banks of the Missouri River at Franklin, Missouri, and crossed Kansas southwesterly to Raton Pass and into Santa Fe in 1821. During the American-Mexican War in 1846, Stephen W. Kearny led his troops over Raton Pass to fight for New Mexico's ownership. In the mid-1840s, Captain John Fremont took his men to evaluate Raton Pass as a possible railroad route.

In 1865, "Uncle Dick" Wootten, one of the early trappers and mountain guides, was asked to build and operate a toll road over Raton Pass. It is reported that he improved the existing twenty-seven mile road from Trinidad, Colorado, to Raton, New Mexico. He operated his toll road from 1865 until 1878 when he sold it to the Atchison, Topeka and Santa Fe Railway. The A.T. and S.F. Railroad built their standard gauge rails over Raton Pass using a short tunnel near the summit. They added a second set of rails during the six year period of 1900 to 1906. In 1908, they built a new two track tunnel and closed the single track tunnel. The border line between Colorado and New Mexico is at the middle of today's railroad tunnel. A good automobile road over Raton Pass was in daily use by 1916.

Conclusion

The War Between the States was fought from 1861 to 1865. The formal Emancipation Proclamation was signed on January 1, 1863. On November 8, 1864, Abraham Lincoln was re-elected President of the United States. He was assassinated on April 14, 1865. The Civil War ended with General Lee's surrender.

Are you wondering what the Civil War had to do with Colorado mountain passes? Refugees and survivors left their destroyed homes and towns in the war zone to start a new life in the West. They came to the mountains of Colorado to search for gold, silver, work, health, and peace. They needed passes to get the roads to cross the mountains, so they built the roads and named the passes. They built towns and started farms and ranches.

There are other passes that were used in the settling of Colorado. I chose to use ninety-two passes that were built for and used by wheeled vehicles. Rick and I hope that you will enjoy our photographs and the words of the many historians that are in our history book.

Bibliography

Abbott, Carl. *Colorado: A History of the Centennial State.* Boulder: Colorado Associated University Press, 1976. Print.

Albi, Charles and Kenton Forrest. *The Moffat Tunnel: A Brief History.* Golden: Colorado Railroad Museum, 1986. Print.

Anderson, Paul, and Ken Johnson. *Elk Mountain Odyssey.* Carbondale: Redstone Press, 1998. Print.

Arps, Louisa W., and Elinor E. Kingery. *High Country Names—Rocky Mountain Park.* Boulder: Johnson Publishing, 1972. Print.

Athearn, Robert. *The Denver and Rio Grande: Rebel of the Rockies.* Lincoln: University of Nebraska Press, 1977. Print.

Beebe, Lucius, and Charles Clegg. *Rio Grande: Main Line of the Rockies.* San Diego: Howell-North, 1962. Print.

Bird, Isabella. *A Lady's Life in the Rocky Mountains.* USA: Barnes and Noble, 2005. Print.

Boner, Harold A. *The Giants Ladder: David Moffat and his railroad.* Milwaukee: Kalmbach Pub. Co., 1992. Print.

Bright, William. *Colorado Place Names.* Boulder: Johnson Printing Company, 1993. Print.

Brown, Robert L. *Ghost Towns of the Colorado Rockies.* Caldwell: Caxton Press , 1990. Print.

Brown, Robert L. *Jeep Trails to Colorado Ghost Towns.* Caldwell : Caxton Printers Ltd., 1963. Print.

Bueler, Gladys R. *Colorado's Colorful Characters.* Boulder: Pruett Publishing Co., 1981. Print.

Cafky, Morris. *Colorado Midland.* Denver: Rocky Mountain Railroad Club, 1965. Print.

Caldwell, John. *George R. Stewart.* Boise: Boise State Univ., 1981. Print.

Collman, McCoy, and Graves. *The RGS Story: The Rio Grande Southern Railroad, Vol. 4.* Denver: Sundance, 1994. Print.

BIBLIOGRAPHY

Colorado Heritage-The Magazine of History. Colorado Center. Denver. 2012.

Crofutt, George A. *Crofutt's Grip Sack Guide of Colorado.* Omaha: Overland Publishing, 1885. Print.

Danielson, Clarence L. and Ralph W. *Basalt: Colorado Midland Town.* Woody Creek: People's Press, 1965,1971, and 2009. Print.

Delorme Atlas & Gazetter. *Colorado Topographic Maps.* (10th ed.) 2011.

Dyer, John L. *An Autobiography; The Snowshoe Itinerant.* Cincinnati: Cranston & Stowe, 1890. Print.

Edmondson, Clyde and Chloe. *Mountain Passes: Location and Information about Mountain Passes, Including Adventure Roads, Scenic Drives and Places of Interest In Colorful Colorado.* Boulder: Estey Printing, 1963. Print.

Ferrell, Mallory Hope. *Silver San Juan: The Rio Grande Southern Railroad.* Boulder: Pruett Publishing Co., 1973. Print.

Fielder, John and Noel. *Colorado: 1870-2000 AD Revisited: The History behind the Images.* Englewood: Westcliff Pub., 2001. Print.

Fossett, Frank. *Colorado: It's Silver and Gold Mines, Farms & Stock Ranges, and Health and Pleasure Resorts: Tourist's Guide to the Rocky Mountains.* NY, NY.: C.G. Crawford, 1880. Print.

Frazier, Deborah. *Colorado's Hot Springs.* Boulder: Pruett Pub. Co.,1996. Print.

Gregory, Doris H. *The History of Colona and Pioneer Families.* 2003. Print.

Griffiths, Mel, and Lynnell Rubright. *Colorado: A Geography.* Boulder: Westview Press, Inc, 1983. Print.

Hafen, Leroy R. and Ann. *Our State: Colorado; a History of Progress.* Denver: Old West Publishing, Co., 1971. Print.

Halka, Chronic. *Roadside Geology of Colorado.* Missoula: Mountain Press, 1986. Print.

Helmers, Dow. *Historic Alpine Tunnel.* Colorado Spgs.: Century One Press, 1971. Print.

Helmouth, Ed and Gloria. *The Passes of Colorado: An Encyclopedia of Watershed Divides.* Boulder: Pruett Publishing Co., 1994. Print.

The Historical Guide to Routt County. Steamboat Springs: Routt County Board of County Commissioners, 1979. Print.

Jackson, Helen Hunt. *Westward to A High Mountain: The Colorado Writings of Helen Hunt Jackson.* Edited Mark I. West. 1994. Print.

Jessen, Kenneth. *Ghost Towns: Colorado Style.* Vol. 3 volumes. 1998. Loveland: J.V. Publications, 1998. Print.

BIBLIOGRAPHY

Jocknick, Sidney. *Early Days on the Western Slope of Colorado.* Ouray: Western Reflections, Inc., 1998. Print.

Kaplan, Michael. *Otto Mears: Paradoxical Pathfinder.* Silverton: San Juan County Book Co., 1982. Print.

Klusmire, Jon. *Colorado.* Oakland: Compass American Guides, 1992. Print.

Koch, Don. *The Colorado Pass Book: A Guide to Colorado's Back Road Mountain Passes.* Boulder: Pruett Publishing Co., 1980. Print.

Lemassena, Robert A. *Rio Grande—To The Pacific.* Sundance Limited. 1974. Print

Leyendecker, Liston, Christine Bradley, and Duane Smith. *The Rise of the Silver Queen.* University Press of Colorado. 2005.

Markalunas, Jim. *Aspen Memories: Recollections of Aspen.* Glenwood Springs: Gran Farnum Printing & Pub., 2010. Print.

Marrifield, Charlotte, and Suzy Kelly. *Memories of St. Elmo.* Evergreen: C. Merrifield, 1992. Print.

Marsh, Charles S. *People of the Shining Mountains.* Boulder: Pruett Publishing Co., 1982. Print.

Massey, Peter, and Jeanne Wilson. *4WD Trails: North Central Colorado.* Castle Rock: Swagman Pub. Co., 1999. Print.

McCollum, Jr., Oscar. *Marble: A Town Built on Dreams.* Denver: Sundance Publications, Ltd. , 1992. Print.

McCoy, Dell, and Russ Collman. *The Rio Grande Pictorial 1871-1971: One Hundred Years of Railroading Through the Rockies.* Denver: Sundance Limited, 1971. Print.

McCoy, Dell, and Russ Collman. *The Crystal River Pictorial.* Denver: Sundance Limited, 1972. Print.

McFarland, Edward M. *Midland Route: A Colorado Midland Guide and Data Book.* Denver: Pruett Pub. Co., 1980. Print.

McTighe, James. *Roadside History of Colorado.* Boulder: Johnson Printing Company, 1984. Print.

Merriam-Webster's Collegiate Dictionary. (10th ed.). (1993). Spring Field, MA: Merriam-Webster.

Moore, George E. *Mines, Mountain, Roads, and Rocks: Guide Book, Geologic Road Logs of the Ouray Area.* Ouray: Ouray Historical Society, 2004. Print.

Morgan, Gary. *Three Foot Rails; A Quick History of the Colorado Central Railroad.* Colo. Springs: Little London Press, 1974. Print.

Noel, Thomas J., Paul F. Mahoney, and Richard E. Stevens. *Historical Atlas of Colorado.* Norman: Univ. of Oklahoma Press, 1994. Print.

BIBLIOGRAPHY

Norton, Boyd and Barbara. *Back Roads of Colorado.* New York: Ruggles Delatour, Inc., 1986. Print.

Norwood, John B. *Rio Grande Narrow Gauge.* River Forest: Heimburger House Pub. Co., 1983. Print.

Ormes, Robert. *Tracking Ghost Railroads in Colorado: A Five Part Guide to Abandoned and Scenic Lines.* Colorado Springs.: Century One Press, 1975. Print.

Parkison, Angela K. *Hope and Hot Water: Glenwood Springs from 1870 to 1891.* Glenwood Springs: Glenwood Springs Legacy Publishing, 2000. Print.

Perry, Eleanor A., and Newton V. Cole. *I Remember Tin Cup: A Trip Back Through Time with Unpublished Stories about the Famous Gold Mining Town, Tincup, Colorado.* Littleton: E. Perry, 1986. Print.

Paulson, Don (Editor). *Narrow Gauge Railroading in the San Juan Triangle.* Ridgway Railroad Museum. 2010.

Pettit, Jan. *Utes; The Mountain People.* Boulder: Johnson Printing Co., 1990. Print.

Poor, Meredith C. *Denver, South Park and Pacific.* Denver: Rocky Mountain Railroad Club, 1976. Print.

Rasmussen, Stephen. *The Rio Grande's La Veta Pass Route.* Burlington: Evergreen Press, 2000. Print.

Rennicke, Jeff. *Colorado Mountain Ranges.* Billings: Falcon Press, 1986. Print.

Rennicke, Jeff. *The Rivers of Colorado.* Billings: Falcon Press, 1985. Print.

Shoemaker, Len. *The Roaring Fork Valley: An Illustrated Chronicle.* Denver: Sundance Limited, 1973. Print.

Smith, P. David. *Mountains of Silver: The Story of Colorado's Red Mountain Mining District.* Ouray: Western Reflections Pub. Co., 2000. Print.

Smith, P. David. *The Road that Silver Built: The Million Dollar Highway.* Lake City: Western Reflections Pub. Co., 2009. Print.

Spitzer, Rick. *Colorado Mountain Passes: The State's Most Accessible High Country Roadways.* Boulder: Westcliffe Publishers, 2009. Print.

Sprague, Marshall. *The Great Gates: The Story of the Rocky Mountain Passes.* Canada: Little Brown, 1964. Print.

Stone, Irving. *Men to Match My Mountains.* New York: Doubleday, 1936. Print.

Taylor, Ralph C. *Colorado South of the Border.* Denver: Sage Books, 1963. Print.

Thode, Jackson C. *George L. Beam and the Denver and Rio Grande, Vol. One.* Denver: Sundance Publications, 1986. Print.

Vandenbusche, Duane, and Rex Myers. *Marble, Colorado: City of Stone.* Denver: Golden Bell Press, 1980. Print.

Vandenbusche, Duane. *The Gunnison Country.* Gunnison: B&B Printers, 1980. Print.

Waldman, Carl. *Biographical Dictionary of American Indian History to 1900; A Biographical Dictionary.* New York: Checkmark Books, 2001. Print.

Wells, Charles A. *Guide to Colorado Back Roads and Four-Wheel Drive Trails Vol. 1 and 2.* Colorado Springs: Fun Treks Inc., 1998-1999. Print.

Wiatrowski, Claude A. *Railroads of Colorado: Your Guide to Colorado's Historic Trains and Railway Sites.* Stillwater: Voyager Press, 2002. Print.

Williamson, Ruby. *Otto Mears: Pathfinder of the San Juan; His Family and Friends.* Buena Vista: R.G. Williamson, 1981. Print.

Wilson, O. Meredith. *The Denver and Rio Grande Project, 1870-1901: A History of the First Thirty Years of the Denver and Rio Grande Railroad.* Salt Lake City: Howe Brothers, 1982. Print.

Wolle, Muriel Sibell. *Stampede to Timberline.* Denver: Self Published, Anteraft Press, 1949. Print.

The WPA Guide to 1930s Colorado. University Press of Kansas, 1987. Print.

Index

Alpine Station & Tunnel 27, 80, 146, 155
Altman's Pass 144
Anza, Gov. Juan Bautista de 39, 151, 156, 160, 164
Argentine Central Railroad 93-94
Argentine Pass 19, 91-92
Ashley, William H. 11-12

Baker, Charles 12, 130-131
Baxter, C.O. 38
Baxter Pass 38
Berthoud, Edward Louis 41, 55-56, 90, 94
Berthoud Pass 55-56
Bird, Isabella L. 94
Black Bear Pass 17, 115-116
Black Sage Pass 149
Blue Mesa Summit 60
Boreas Pass 99-100
Breckinridge, John C. 100
Breckenridge, Town of 100-101
Bridger, Jim 41, 47, 55-56, 90, 94
Bridal Veil Falls 116
Buffalo Pass 43-44
Busk Tunnel Railway Company 63
Byers, William N. 56

Cabin Creek Hydroelectric Plant 94-95
California Gulch 20
Cameron Pass 50
Cameron, Robert A. 50
Camp Bird 21, 118
Camp Hale 86
Canyon Pintado 40
Carson, Kit 102, 136, 143, 157
Cerro Summit 61
Cinnamon Pass 21, 129-130
Climax-Henderson Molybedenum Mine 22, 58, 85
Coal Bank and Molas Passes 126-127
Cochetopa Pass 139-140

Colorado Central Railroad 25, 90
Colorado Mineral Belt 18-19
Colorado Midland Railroad 20, 62, 87, 108, 110, 143
Colorado's Minerals 18-22
Como 100
Cordova Pass 162-163
Cottonwood Pass One 88-89
Cottonwood Pass Two (South of Gypsum) 62
Cripple Creek 20
Crooke Brothers 76
Crystal City 69
Crystal River Railroad 70
Cucharas Pass 163-164
Cumberland Pass 20, 79-80
Cumbres Pass 165-166
Currant Creek Pass 108-109

Dallas Divide 114-115
Decatur, Stephen 91
Denver, Northwestern and Pacific Railway 54
Denver and Rio Grande Railroad 20, 23-25, 70, 74, 84-87, 108-109, 113, 130, 133, 135, 142, 153, 158, 161, 164, 166
Denver, South Park and Pacific Railroad 20, 25, 54, 75-76, 78, 80-81, 85, 87, 100, 102-103, 144, 146-147, 154-155
Dominguez, Father Francisco 9, 12, 39, 114
Dotsero Cutoff 34
Douglas Pass 39-40
Douglas, Ute Indian Chief 42
Dunckley Pass 43
Dyer, John L. 43, 101, 103-106

Elgin, Charles 80-81
Elwood Pass 137-138
Engineer Pass 127-128, 135

INDEX

Escalante, Father Silvestre 9, 12, 39, 114
Evans, Dr. John 25-26, 54, 56, 85, 100, 144
Evans, James A. 26, 46, 103, 144

Fall River Pass 52-53
Fremont Indians 40
Fremont Pass 84-85
Fremont, Lt. John 13, 44, 46, 60, 84-85, 98, 102, 142, 157

Galloping Goose 31-32
Georgetown, Town of 18, 93, 96
Georgia Pass 98-99
Gibbs, Charles W. 31
Gillespie, H. B. 20, 72
Gilson, Samuel 38
Golden Gate Pass 56-57
Golden, Tom 56
Gore Pass 46
Gore, Sir St. George 46-47
Grant, Ulysses S. 68-69
Gregory, John 18, 56
Griffith, David and George 18, 93, 96
Guanella, Byron 95
Guanella Pass 94-95
Gunnison, Captain John 13, 60-61, 139-140, 152, 157-158, 160
Guy, John 57

Hagerman, James J. 28, 62, 110, 143
Hagerman Pass 62-64
Hagerman Tunnel 64
Hamill, William A. 96
Hancock Pass 147-148
Harrison, President B. H. 7
Hayden, Ferdinand V. 14, 20, 42, 68, 86
Hayden Pass 153
Hill, Nathan P. 18
Hoosier Pass 101-102
Hotchkiss, Enos 21, 133, 135
Huff, James 19, 93, 96

Imogene Pass 21, 114, 118
Independence Mining Camp 65

Independence Pass 20, 64-66

Jackson, George A. 18, 56
Jackson, William H. 42, 63, 83, 136
Jones Pass 57
Jones, John S. 57-58

Kebler, John 73
Kebler Pass 73-74
Kenosha Pass 102-103
King, Clarence 14
King, Ira 65

La Manga Pass 164
La Poudre Pass 7, 50-51
La Salle Pass 109
La Salle, Samuel 109
La Veta Pass 160-162
Lake City, Town of 133, 135
Leadville, Town of 20, 87
Lizard Head Pass 119-120
Long, Major Stephen H. 13
Los Piños Pass 16, 136
Lotis, Fred 71, 77
Loveland Pass 83, 90-91
Loveland, William A. H. 25, 90-91, 94

Marble Quarry 69-70
Marshall Pass 152-153
Marvine, Archibald 42, 44, 46
Mary Murphy Mine 155
McClure Pass 66
McClure, Thomas "Mack" 66
Mears, Otto 15-17, 21, 30-31, 60-61, 113-115, 117, 119, 121-122, 124-125, 130, 133, 135-136, 152-153
Medano Pass 156-158
Meeker, Nathan 10-11, 42
Middle Park 7
Milner Pass 51
Milner, T. J. 51
Moffat, David Halliday, Jr. 32, 54
Moffat Tunnel 32-34
Molas Pass, see Coal Bank Pass
Monarch Pass 150-151

178

INDEX

Mosquito Pass Toll Road 106
Mosquito Pass 20, 103
Mount of the Holy Cross 84
Muddy Pass 44-45

North Cochetopa Pass 139
North La Veta Pass 60, 157
North Park 6
Nunn, Lucien L. 116, 119-120

Ohio Pass 75-76
Ophir Loop 31
Ophir Pass 120-122
Ouray, Chief 10-11, 136
Ouray, Town of 113-114
Owl Creek Pass 112-113

Palisades 146
Palmer Divide 142
Palmer, William J. 23, 142, 153, 161
Pass Creek Pass 159
Pearl Pass 70-71
Pike, Lt. Zebulon 13, 64, 102, 108-109, 157
Pitkin 81
Poncha Pass 151-152
Powell, Major John Wesley 14

Rabbit Ears Pass 44
Rainbow Route 16
Raton Pass 166
Red Hill Pass 103
Red Mountain Mining District 21, 30
Red Mountain Pass 123-125
Ridgway, R. M. 31
Rio Grande Southern Railroad 31-32, 115, 117, 119, 121-122
Robidoux, Antoine 60-61, 140
Robinson, John 21
Rollins, John Q. A. 53, 107
Rollins Pass 53-54
Rollinsville 53
Romley, Hancock, Towns of 155
Russell, William Green 18

Sage, Rufus B. 45-46
Sangre de Cristo, name of 160
Sangre de Cristo Pass 159-160
San Luis Valley 7
Saunders, James 36
Schofield, B. F. 68
Schofield Pass 68-70
Senter, Charles 21, 85
Shrine Pass 83-84
Silverton Gladstone and Northerly Railroad 30, 130
Silverton Northern Railroad 30
Silverton Railroad 30, 124-125, 130
Silverton, Town of 21, 130
Slumgullion Pass 132-133
South Park 7
Spencer, Gen. George 100
Spring Creek Pass 134-135
Steele, R. W. 19, 96
St. Elmo, Town of 20, 144, 154-155
Stony Pass 131

Tabor, H. A. W. 56, 87
Taylor, Jim 71-72
Taylor Pass 20, 71-72
Taylor, Robert 19, 96
Telluride, Town of 21, 116, 117
Tennessee Pass 86
Tesla, Nikola 116, 120
Thornburgh, Maj. Thomas 42
Tincup Pass 20, 77
Tincup Town 77-79
Tomichi Pass 148-149
Trout Creek Pass 107-108

Ulibari, Captain Juan 12, 164
Ute Indians 9, 10, 40
Ute Pass One (near Colo. Springs) 28, 143
Ute Pass Two (Off Hwy. 9) 58

Vail, Charles D. 83, 151
Vail Pass 83
Virginia City 78

INDEX

Waldorf Mining and Milling Company 93
Walsh, Tom 21, 114, 118
Waunita Hot Springs 80
Waunita Pass 80-81
Webster Pass 97
Webster, William and Emerson 97
Westinghouse, George 116, 120
Weston, Algernon and Philo 106
Weston Pass 106
Wheeler, B. Clark 20, 65
Wheeler, Lt. George 14, 54, 152-153
Wilcox, Edward J. 93
Wilkerson, John 110
Wilkerson Pass 110
Williams, "Old" Bill Williams 143, 145
Williams Pass 145-146
Willow Creek Pass 49
Wolf Creek Pass 137
Womack, William and Robert 20
Wood, Dave 89
Woods, Alvinus 20
Wooton, "Uncle" Dick 166

Yankee Girl Mine 16, 21, 123-124
Yellow Jacket Pass 41-42
Yule, George 69
Yule Marble Company 70